Called Together

Called Together

*Asks the difficult questions that all couples
must answer before and after they say "I do."
Prepares you for a successful marriage
through unique couple-to-couple mentoring.*

STEVE AND MARY PROKOPCHAK

DESTINY IMAGE® PUBLISHERS, INC.
P.O. Box 310, Shippensburg, PA 17257–0310

"Speaking to the Purposes of God for this Generation and for the Generations to Come."

This book and all other Destiny Image, Revival Press, Mercy Place, Fresh Bread, Destiny Image Fiction, and Treasure House books are available at Christian bookstores and distributors worldwide.

For a U.S. bookstore nearest you, call 1–800–722–6774.
For more information on foreign distributors, call 717–532–3040.
Or reach us on the Internet: www.destinyimage.com.

Previously Revised Edition ©1999, 2003 by Steve and Mary Prokopchak
Updated Edition: ©2007 ISBN: 978–0–87509–991–0
ISBN 10: 0–7684–2738–XISBN 13: 978–0–7684–2738–7

For Worldwide Distribution, Printed in the U.S.A.
1 2 3 4 5 6 7 8 9 10 11 / 13 12 11 10 09

Dedication

This premarital training book is dedicated
first to the author of marriage, our Lord Jesus Christ,
and second to our children, Joshua, Marc, and Brooke,
wonderful blessings from our call together.

Endorsements

Called Together tackles the difficult questions that couples must face before and after marriage. While some premarital materials take the easy road, this one takes the best road—the real-life road.

Thomas Whiteman, PhD
Author, Founder, and President of Life Counseling and
Director of "Fresh Start" Divorce Recovery Seminars

If a marriage is to stand the test of the challenges life brings, it needs to be built on a solid foundation. *Called Together* is a great tool assisting couples preparing for marriage to lay such a foundation. Presenting Christ-centered principles, it also equips couples to build healthy and fulfilling marriages on this foundation.

Tomasz Ropiejko, Pastor/Counselor
Pentecostal Church of Poland

Called Together is a practical, helpful, and biblically based guidebook for preparing couples for marriage, as well as for helping them grow together in the first year of marriage. I recommend it highly.

Rev. Siang-Yang Tan, PhD
Senior Pastor, First Evangelical Church of Glendale, California
Professor of Psychology, Fuller Seminary

Spending time working through and discussing issues raised in this book was a wonderful way of preparing sensibly for our marriage, especially since we come from two countries that look at marriage in different ways. We consider *Called Together* essential for any couple preparing for marriage, all the more so if they come from different cultures.

Peter and RuthAnn Bunton
Overseers, DOVE Mission International

We have a young church, and several years ago there was a tide of weddings in it. The *Called Together* book by Steve and Mary Prokopchak was a great asset to the ministry. In fact, the family ministry of our church began because of their book. Premarital counseling was a foreign concept at that time in Russia, and *Called Together* gave us much freedom to address specific challenges a couple might face, providing discussion topics applicable to every situation.

Vlad and Natasha Zuev
Director of Family Ministries
Vyborg, Russia

Steve and Mary Prokopchak have written one of the most helpful books available on marriage. We use it in our church for all of our premarital counseling, plus many of our married couples have found it extremely helpful when they need a boost in their relationship. I highly recommend this practical, biblical, and very insightful book.

Floyd McClung
Cape Town, South Africa
International Director, All Nations

As a professional marriage counselor and pastor, I feel this biblically based resource is of great value in preparing engaged couples for a successful marriage. It encourages honesty and stimulates open communication.

Steve Lalor
Marriage Counselor and Pastor

We have been using the *Called Together* materials for all of our premarital and postmarital counseling, and have found it both practical and comprehensive. It's a tool we could not do without!

Reverend Ibrahim Omondi
DOVE Africa Apostolic Leader, Nairobi, Kenya

Contents

Foreword

With the myriad of marriages failing in America, every engaged couple needs to consider how to improve its odds of having a lifelong marriage. Fortunately, it *is* possible to get "marriage insurance"—drastically improving the likelihood that their marriage will go the distance—*if* couples take several proven steps in advance of the wedding. What are those steps?

Based on my reporting in a nationally syndicated column, "Ethics and Religion," since 1981 and my work as president of an organization called Marriage Savers, I have come across the five most important steps a seriously dating or engaged couple can take to prepare for a great marriage. All of them are in *Called Together*, written by an experienced mentoring couple, the Prokopchaks.

1. Do not cohabit. According to the University of Wisconsin's National Survey of Families and Households, 40 out of 100 couples who cohabit separate before a wedding, and 45 out of the 60 remaining will divorce, leaving only 15 out of 100 couples together after ten years.

2. Remain chaste. The sexually experienced have divorce rates two-thirds higher than those who are not, according to a key study.

3. Take a premarital inventory to get an objective view of strengths and weaknesses.

4. Be mentored by an older couple who can help engaged couples talk through issues that counseling brings up.

5. Use a book such as *Called Together* to learn biblical principles about how to build a lifelong marriage. This book that you hold in your hands can have a profound impact on you as a person, as a future husband or wife, and as a parent. It will require a lot of quiet study of Scripture, and honest self-assessment of your communication and conflict resolution skills, and knowledge of yourself, your partner, and your relationship that few couples acquire by simply dating.

Most young people look *for* the "perfect mate," but what the Prokopchaks are saying is that you must *be* the perfect mate. You must work on the many ways you can build a marriage on the solid rock of Christ. If you do so, and continue to invest energy and commitment, the Prokopchaks and I believe you will have an enduring marriage that brings glory to God and to your children and grandchildren.

Mike McManus
President, Marriage Savers

****

During 1970, my wife, LaVerne, and I had the privilege of ministering to hundreds of young people each week. It was a sheer joy witnessing the grace of God in these young lives. They were young radicals who had chosen to give their all to build the Kingdom of God. Eventually these young men and women began to establish meaningful relationships. The next step was marriage.

In 1980, we obeyed the Lord's call to pioneer a new church filled with many of these same young people. We tried our best to teach them practical biblical principles to properly prepare them for this massive step—two becoming one in "holy matrimony." In retrospect, the instruction given to these young couples during those days was "weighed in the scales and found wanting."

Steve Prokopchak joined our team in 1987 and began to develop a counseling ministry for this new church. I was impressed with Steve's ability to trust the Word of God and the Holy Spirit as he gave clear biblical and practical counseling. He spoke into people's lives with compassion. After many years of writing and rewriting, *Called Together* emerged. The results have been tremendous!

A practical, insightful, and helpful book, *Called Together* has revolutionized premarital and postmarital counseling in our network of churches. We have seen these scriptural principles worked out in the lives of the authors and in hundreds of engaged and married couples. With its clear biblical approach, *Called Together* helps engaged couples come face-to-face with real issues that they will confront throughout their lives together.

Requests from pastors and counselors for *Called Together* materials have come from five continents.

Thank you, Steve and Mary, for allowing the Lord to use you to help prepare engaged couples for marriage in a way that is scriptural and down-to-earth. May our Lord Jesus Christ be praised!

Larry and LaVerne Kreider
International Director
DOVE Christian Fellowship International
Lititz, Pennsylvania

Introduction

Traveling in many different countries of the world, we have discovered that few churches engage in adequate preparation and training for marriage. If marriage was introduced by the God that we know and love, shouldn't the Christian church take the mandate of "two becoming one" more seriously? Couples spend 200-plus hours preparing for a one-day ceremony; and yet, this ceremony does nothing to build a couple's foundation for a lifetime together.

When we train premarital and postmarital counselors we often ask, "Did you receive premarital training?" The replies are frequently humorous. Some couples tell us they cannot remember. (What an impact their counseling had on them!) Others say "yes," but they cannot remember how many sessions were held. Even fewer couples can recall what was taught while attending premarital sessions with their pastor. One couple told us they had two sessions and then were forced to quit. When asked why, the couple said, "We were seeing a psychologist and could no longer afford to pay for the counseling."

When we, the authors, announced our engagement, the next item on our agenda was scheduling premarital counseling with our pastor. Our one and only session was held in the pastor's home with only the pastor present. Our session lasted 45 minutes, and the only topic we can recall was that of submission.

As we look back, we realize that most churches were following the same format in the 1970s; our premarital counseling was average or even better than what some couples received—none.

In retrospect, we wish that we could have had a mentoring couple to come alongside us, to share with us, pray with us, encourage us, and hold us accountable in our relationship before and after the wedding day.

It is our desire to see couples trained in pre- and postmarital counseling principles to the honor and glory of God. We believe that the results of this training will validate our reasons for offering this course of study.

This book is to be provocative by nature. It is designed to challenge you into wholehearted, Christ-centered commitment or to cause you to rethink your decision for marriage.

Called Together is best facilitated couple-to-couple, a counselor couple with a premarital couple. Michael McManus, in his book *Marriage Savers*, advocates the couple-to-couple mentoring approach when he states, "No one is better equipped to help...than a seasoned, mature couple with a solid marriage." He adds, "Mentor couples can be practical role models to other couples and give precious time that the pastor does not have. Such people are the greatest untapped resource for saving marriages."[1]

We would like to present six reasons for premarital education: (1) maintaining a realistic perspective during the engagement period; (2) developing marital skills; (3) provoking serious thought concerning a lifelong commitment; (4) preventing problems in the future; (5) assessing the present relationship; (6) developing goals and long-term vision for the covenant relationship.

The home is the basic unit of the Kingdom of God. As the home is established and restored, so will the Kingdom of God be established and restored. We desire to see the Kingdom of God established in every nation. This long-term vision will unfold as men and women of God, as families, are called together and then are called to go to the uttermost parts of the earth. This course is for you if you are engaged to be married, if you are planning marriage someday, if you are considering remarriage, or if you are newly married.

Endnote

1. Michael J. McManus, *Marriage Savers* (Grand Rapids, MI: Zondervan, 1995).

Congratulations!

Congratulations to the two of you in your desire to spend your lives together serving God.

We appreciate your willingness to be involved in premarital education. This course is designed to prepare you for God's call to marriage. These will be some of the most important counseling sessions in which you will ever be involved. Marriage preparation counseling must be a time of thorough searching and communication concerning your past, your present, and your dreams for the future.

In preparation for your first session, please carefully and prayerfully complete the following items: "Premarital Counseling Information," "Spiritual Overview," "About Me," and "A Biblical Concept of Love." "A Biblical Concept of Love" is the only assignment you will work on together. You may complete the assignment "Who I Am in Christ" at your own pace.

Please take all of your assignments seriously, complete them thoroughly, and turn them in to your counselors before your actual counseling session. This will aid your counselors in preparation for the session and help you complete the counseling process smoothly. Even before this process is finished, you will see an improvement in the quality of your relationship. After you are married, you will understand more fully the purpose of preparation for marriage by building a thorough foundation.

Expect a meaningful experience. Be prepared for loving, honest, and challenging counselors. Do not hesitate to ask relevant questions of each other and your counselors. God bless you in your call together!

Preliminary Information

Personal Identification

Name _____

Address _____

City _____

State _____ Zip code_____

Phone (Home)

Phone (Cell)

Occupation

Sex

Birth Date

Premarital Status:

     Single

     Separated

     Divorced

     Widowed

Education (Circle last year completed)

     High School 8 9 10 11 12   College 1 2 3 4 5 6 +

Do you have children?

     Name

     Age

     Sex

Living with you?

     Name

     Age

     Sex

Living with you?

     Name

     Age

     Sex

Living with you?

Health Information

Rate your physical health:

Very good _____ Good _____ Average_____ Declining _____ Other

Your approximate weight ___lbs.

Recent weight changes: Lost _____ Gained _____

List important present or past illnesses: _____

Date of last medical exam: _____

Your physician: _____

Address: _____

Have you used drugs for other than medical purposes? Yes _____ No _____

Are you presently taking medication? Yes _____ No _____

Have you ever had a severe emotional upset? Yes _____ No _____

Have you ever had any psychotherapy or individual counseling? Yes _____
No _____

Have you ever had an abortion? Yes _____ No _____

As a male, have you ever been involved in a relationship in which an abortion was performed to terminate a pregnancy? Yes _____ No _____

Religious Background

Do you consider yourself a Christian? Yes___ No ___

If yes, did you accept Christ as your Savior? Yes___ No___

Do you have a regular devotional time? Yes___ No___

Are you engaging in family or individual worship/devotion?
Yes ___ No ___

Explain any recent changes or problems with your spiritual walk.

_____

Personality

Have you ever suffered from depression? Yes _____ No _____

If yes, when? _____

Have you ever been involved in a cult, the occult, astrology, etc.? Yes _____ No _____

Explain _____

Do you fear anything? (e.g., are you afraid of the dark, dying, the loss of a parent, etc.?) _____

Marriage Information
(if previously married)

How long did you know your former spouse before marriage? _____

Length of engagement _____

Is your previous spouse deceased? Yes _____ No _____

Did you divorce? Yes _____ No _____ When did this occur?

Did you receive premarital instruction? Yes_____ No _____

Parental History

Were you raised by your natural parents? Yes _____ No _____

Are your parents still living? Yes _____ No _____

What is/was your parents' religious affiliation? (e.g., Methodist, Catholic, etc.)

Are/were they Christians? Yes _____ No _____

Are your parents still living together? Yes _____ No _____

If your parents are separated or divorced, when did this occur? _____

Rate your parents' marriage: Happy ___ Average ___ Unhappy ___

As a child, did you feel closest to your: Father __ Mother __ Other ___

Was your childhood: Happy _____ Average _____ Unhappy _____

How many brothers and sisters do you have? Brothers __ Sisters ___

What number child were you in the birth order? _____

Other

Is there any other information you think is important? _____

Important: Please elaborate on any area concerning premarital education that you would like to see covered. The following are some examples to help you identify specific areas of concern: different cultural backgrounds, social activities, future plans, employment, finances, parents or future in-laws, physical boundaries during engagement, bad habits, conflict in communication, wedding plans, etc. Other areas of concern:_____

Before You Marry: Premarital Section

About Me

Taking an honest and intimate look at yourself and your partner is fundamental to the development and maintenance of unity within your marriage relationship. This session will challenge you to explore and understand yourself more fully.

It is imperative that each of you responds to the questions with your own book. Sharing a book allows one of you the opportunity to read the other's response and will skew your responses. Total dedication to honesty throughout this book is extremely important. Not to be totally honest could have a harmful effect upon your future together.

When you and your partner come together with your premarital counselors, you will be given the opportunity to share about yourself and listen to your partner. Understanding one another will be a continuing process during your marriage relationship. Some of the most important foundational material will be discussed in this session. Speak truthfully and listen intently.

We encourage you to be honest as you answer the following questions and complete the open-ended statements. Allow this first session to be a meaningful experience for each of you.

There is one other issue we would like to present to you as you prepare for your wedding day. Perhaps you may feel that it is too soon to think about this, but we hope you will consider our advice after years of marital preparation with engaged couples. The wedding day is a special day, but a long day, after months of preparation. We encourage couples to consider wedding ceremonies as early in the day as possible. Your first night together as a married couple is special, and you will need time and energy to enjoy these moments.

Second, we offer you input regarding the honeymoon. We feel it is imperative to plan time together, not just sightseeing or traveling thousands of miles. Honeymoons are when the world stops, you get off and spend quality and quantity time enjoying one another's presence. Many couples reported to us that if they could redo the honeymoon it would involve less doing and more being with the one to whom they made a life commitment.

About Me

Complete the following statements with what first comes to mind. Do this exercise separately.

1.   I see myself as _____

2.   A word that would best describe me is _____

3.   Success in life to me is _____

4.   My strongest quality is _____

5.   One of my weaknesses is _____

6.   Others view me as _____

7.   I become quiet when _____

8.   When others have a different opinion than I do, my reaction is to

   _____

9.   My feelings tend to be hurt when _____

10. I feel guilty when _____

11. I worry when _____

12. I feel accepted when _____

13. What makes me feel inadequate is _____

14. I feel depressed when _____

15. I receive pleasure from _____

16. I am disappointed when _____

17. Some of my gifts include _____

18. My self-confidence falters when _____

19. I get defensive when _____

20. Something that makes me laugh is _____

21. I get angry when _____

22. When angry with someone, I tend to _____

23. I receive great satisfaction from _____

24. I feel trapped when _____

25. I am afraid when _____

Spiritual Overview

Separately, each of you should complete the following statements concerning your spiritual life.

1. My relationship with Jesus Christ is _____

2. My definition of sin is _____

3. Describe how you deal with sin. _____

4. Is Jesus Lord of your life? _____
   Please elaborate. _____

5. Have you been water baptized since accepting Christ? Yes __ No__
   If no, why not? Be prepared to share your experience. _____

   _____

   _____

6. As a believer, what is your experience with the Holy Spirit?

   _____

   _____

7. Describe your prayer life (where? when? why? etc.). _____

   _____

8. I read the Bible (when? for what reasons? etc.) _____

   _____

   _____

9. My personal commitment to attending a church (body of believers) is
   (how often? for what reasons? etc.) _____

   _____

10. My understanding of God is _____

    _____

11. In a spiritual sense, marriage will solve the following problems:

    _____

    _____

12. I would like to make the following change(s) in my spiritual life:

    _____

    _____

    _____

    _____

Individual Mission

Complete this assignment alone. What you express will be your individual desire and call from God.

Jesus came to do the will of the Father who sent Him (see John 6:38). God also has a plan for your life. Read First Corinthians 12:12-20,27, and write about what you see as God's mission for you. For example, you may believe God wants you to be a youth leader, Sunday school teacher, business owner, mother, or foreign missionary. God has a destiny for each of us. Take the time to write about what you see as your destiny.

_____

_____

_____

_____

_____

_____

_____

_____

_____

_____

_____

_____

_____

_____

_____

_____

_____

_____

_____

_____

_____

_____

_____

Biblical Concept of Love

Take the necessary time to read and study this exercise together. The following Scripture references, along with a word study on the three types of love, provide an overview of the basic ingredient in healthy family relationships.

Eros – A love that seeks its own. Unlike agape love, it is self–centered, sensual, and inspired by selfish human nature. It is conditional love.

Phileo – A brotherly, friendship, companionship type of love. Phileo denotes mutual attraction, cooperation, and communication between two individuals.

Agape – A self-giving love that does not seek anything in return. It's a love that endures even when another person becomes unlovable. It is like God's love, self-sacrificing and other-centered.

Scriptural Study of Love

Matthew 22:37-39 . . . . Love God first
Luke 6:27-35 . . . . Love your enemies
John 13:34 . . . . Love one another
Romans 13:8-10 . . . . Love is the fulfillment of the law
1 Corinthians 8:1 . . . . Love edifies
Galatians 5:13 . . . . Serve through love
Galatians 6:2 . . . . Bear one another's burdens
Ephesians 4:2 . . . . Bear with one another in love
Ephesians 5:25 . . . . Husbands, love as Christ loved
1 Peter 4:8 . . . . Love covers sins
1 John 3:16-18. Love is laying down your life
1 Corinthians 13. . . . . The most excellent way

The following are questions to ask each other.

1. Many couples experience a decrease in romantic love at some point after they are married. Discuss why you think this may be true and the steps you can take to keep romantic love alive within your marriage.
2. Discuss the difference between "young love" and "old love." What are some of the positives and negatives of both?
3. Take some time to dialogue about how you prefer to receive love. Does it mean more to you to hear the words "I love you," than to see loving acts or to feel love?
4. As a married couple, how do you see yourselves progressing through the three types of love (*eros*, *phileo*, and *agape*)?
5. Consider asking your premarital counselors to share how they progressed through the three types of love.

Sexual Boundaries

As the process of premarital counseling begins, it is important to consider your sexual boundaries. Many couples express that they will not be involved in sexual intercourse, but have not taken the time to communicate beyond this point. The following exercise, to be completed individually, will challenge you to know where your sexual boundaries are. Consequently, you will know when you are approaching the limit you have set for yourselves.

Below is an example of physical progression of intimacy in a relationship:

1. Holding hands
2. Arm around shoulder/waist
3. Embracing
4. Kissing on the cheek
5. Kissing on the lips
6. French kissing
7. Fondling sexual areas
8. Sexual intercourse

Take the time to write your personal responses to the following questions.

1. As an engaged couple, have you discussed your physical boundaries?
   Yes _____ No _____
   Write about physical boundaries as you and your fiancé/ée interpret them.
2. Have you moved beyond these boundaries in your relationship?
   Yes _____ No _____
3. Are you currently living together or have you been involved in cohabitation in the past?
4. My definition of fornication is
5. Discuss the negative impact that fornication may have on your relationship.
6. Are there places that should be "off limits" for you as a couple?
7. Are there times you should not be alone together?
8. First Thessalonians 4:1-8 states God's will for you concerning sexual areas. What is His will?
9. Read Ephesians 5:3-11. How does this Scripture relate to sexual boundaries?
10. How can you relate First Timothy 5:1-2 to your relationship with each other?
11. List the specific steps you can take to prevent sexual impurity.

12. Developing a key word or phrase that indicates you are approaching your physical boundaries is helpful. Prepare for your next premarital session by jotting down some possible key words or phrases.

Now that you have completed this exercise, make a commitment to communicate with each other and your premarital counselors about your personal boundaries. Ask your counselors to help hold you as a couple accountable in the sexual area. Discuss together the following benefits and blessings of maintaining biblical sexual boundaries.

- You will be obeying God and will have His blessing.
- You will build trust toward intimacy within your relationship.
- Maintaining appropriate sexual boundaries affirms the worth of one another. You are showing that you care more about this person than your sexual needs or desires.
- You become an example to your elders and your peers, and will one day have a testimony to share with your children and your grandchildren.
- Waiting to be sexually intimate within marriage will protect you from rejection and other emotional hurts, as well as sexually transmitted diseases.
- Your sexual commitment to one another within marriage will be trust filled because this trust was not broken before marriage.
- You will avoid a possible pregnancy.
- By waiting, your love, respect, and emotions for one another will not be confused with guilt and thinking that is clouded by lust.
- Maintaining your sexual boundaries will build love, respect, self-control, and patience.

Who I Am in Christ

First Thessalonians 5:23 states that we are spirit, soul, and body. Normally, we feed the body three meals a day. The soul is educated and fed emotionally. This exercise is designed to nourish the *spirit*, that part of us in which God dwells. Study these Scriptures together and individually to discover who you are in Christ. Discovering a biblical self-image in Christ increases your dependency upon Him and decreases an unhealthy dependency upon one another.

I am now God's child . . . . 1 John 3:2

I am born of the imperishable seed of God's Word . . . . . 1 Peter 1:23

I am loved by Christ and freed from my sins . . . . Revelation 1:6

I am forgiven all my sins . . . . Ephesians 1:7

I am justified from all things . . . . Acts 13:39

I am the righteousness of God . . . . 2 Corinthians 5:21

I am free from all condemnation . . . . Romans 8:1

I can forget the past . . . . Philippians 3:13

I am a new creature . . . . 2 Corinthians 5:17

I am the temple of the Holy Spirit . . . . 1 Corinthians 6:19

I am redeemed from the curse of the law . . . . Galatians 3:13

I am reconciled to God . . . . 2 Corinthians 5:18

I am beloved of God . . . . 1 John 4:10

I am a saint and loved by God . . . . Romans 1:7

I am holy and without blame before Him . . . . Ephesians 1:4

I am the head and not the tail . . . . Deuteronomy 28:13

I am called of God by the grace given in Christ . . . . . 2 Timothy 1:9

I am brought near by the blood of Christ . . . . Ephesians 2:13

I have been given fullness in Christ . . . . Colossians 2:10

I am delivered from the power of darkness . . . . Colossians 1:13

I am an ambassador for Christ . . . . 2 Corinthians 5:20

I am the salt of the earth . . . . Matthew 5:13

I am the light of the world . . . . Matthew 5:14

I am dead to sin . . . . Romans 6:2

I am alive to God . . . . Romans 6:11

I am raised up with Christ and seated in heavenly realms . Ephesians 2:6

I am a king and a priest to God . . . . Revelation 1:6

I am loved with an everlasting love . . . . Jeremiah 31:3

I am an heir of God and a joint heir with Christ . . . . . Romans 8:17

I am qualified to share in the inheritance of the Kingdom . Colossians 1:12

I am more than a conqueror. . . . . Romans 8:37

I am healed by the wounds of Jesus. . . . . 1 Peter 2:24

I am built on the foundation of the apostles and prophets,
     with Jesus Christ Himself as the chief cornerstone . . Ephesians 2:20

I am in Christ Jesus by God's act . . . . 1 Corinthians 1:30

I am kept by God's power . . . . 1 Peter 1:5

I am sealed with the promised Holy Spirit . . . . Ephesians 1:13

I have everlasting life . . . . John 5:24

I am crucified with Christ, nevertheless I live . . . . . . Galatians 2:20

I am a partaker of the divine nature . . . . 2 Peter 1:4

I have been given all things that pertain to life . . . . 2 Peter 1:3

I have been blessed with every spiritual blessing . . . . . Ephesians 1:3

I have peace with God . . . . Romans 5:1

I am a chosen royal priest . . . . 1 Peter 2:9

I can do all things through Christ . . . . Philippians 4:13

I have all my needs met by God according to His
     riches in glory in Christ Jesus . . . . Philippians 4:19

I shall do even greater works than Christ Jesus . . . . John 14:12

I am being kept strong and blameless to the end . . 1 Corinthians 1:8

I am chosen by Him . . . . 1 Thessalonians 1:4

I overcome the world . . . . 1 John 5:4

I have a guaranteed inheritance . . . . Ephesians 1:14

I am a fellow citizen in God's household . . . . Ephesians 2:19

Christ's truth has set me free . . . . John 8:32

I always triumph in Christ . . . . 2 Corinthians 2:14

I am in Jesus Christ's hands . . . . John 10:28

I am holy, without blemish and free from accusation. Colossians 1:22

Christ in me is the hope of glory . . . . Colossians 1:27

I am anointed by the Holy One . . . . 1 John 2:20

God's love is lavished upon me. 1 John 3:1

He is able to keep me from falling and present me
     without fault. . . . . Jude 24

I am God's house . . . . Hebrews 3:6

God has given me a spirit of power, of love, and
     of self-discipline. . . . . 2 Timothy 1:7

I am convinced that He is able to guard what I
     have entrusted to Him. 2 Timothy 1:12

He considers me faithful and appointed me to

His service..... .... 1 Timothy 1:12

I am justified by faith........................... Romans 3:28

The Spirit Himself intercedes for me............... Romans 8:26

Inwardly I am being renewed day by day .... 2 Corinthians 4:16

For freedom Christ has set me free .... Galatians 5:1

I am held together by Him..................... Colossians 1:17

I have the mind of Christ .... 1 Corinthians 2:16

What verses specifically ministered to my spirit and why?

What verses spoke to the two of us about maintaining a healthy interdependency?

About Us

Many couples enter marriage unrealistically. God wants us to be full of faith but "wise as serpents." With the great wealth of literature, videos, and tapes available to us on the subjects of marriage, sex, finances, communication, and so forth, no couple should enter marriage unaware of satan's devices to undermine and destroy relationships.

Why do you want to marry this particular person? How do you both know that God is calling you together? What are your expectations for this marriage? How would you react to potentially difficult circumstances should they arise during your marriage? Are your parents in agreement with your engagement? Assignments for Session Two address these questions. This session will also help you assess your expectations and perceptions of marriage and will end with the two of you working on a cooperative mission. Please be aware that you will need to copy the "Parent Questionnaire" pages for your parents to complete and turn in to your premarital counselors with other Session Two homework.

God has a perfect design for marriage. When conflicts or difficult circumstances arise, God's Word offers help and hope for each situation.

Reasons for Marriage

1. In your own words, define marriage.
2. Have you thought through your reasons for marrying?
   List ten of those reasons.
   1.
   2.
   3.
   4.
   5.
   6.
   7.

8.

9.

10.

3. What confirmation do you both have that God is calling you together? Please elaborate.

4. Why is this the right time in your life to marry?

5. Marriage is for the mature. List some characteristics and evidences of maturity that you see in each other.

Expectations and Perceptions of Marriage

1. Without each other's help, list ten expectations you will have when you are married. For example, a husband might expect his wife not to be employed outside the home, to balance the checkbook, to mow the lawn, and to perform all household duties. A wife might expect her husband to be the head of the family, to administer all child discipline, to help with housework, and to limit sports activities with his friends.

   1.

   2.

   3.

   4.

   5.

   6.

   7.

   8.

   9.

   10.

2. By yourself, consider your expectations in the area of household chores. Below is a list of chores. Who will be responsible for the completion of these chores? Mark H for husband, W for wife, or S for shared.

   ____ Washing dishes

   ____ Laundry

   ____ Ironing

   ____ Cleaning vehicles

   ____ Washing windows

   ____ Cleaning bathrooms

   ____ Meal preparation

_____ Pet care

_____ Collecting trash

_____ Mowing the lawn

_____ Gardening

_____ Dusting

_____ Vacuuming

_____ Making the bed

_____ Grocery shopping

_____ Vehicle maintenance

When meeting with your premarital counselors, take the time to discuss any differences you discover regarding chore and household expectations.

The following are some tips for you and your fiancé/ée to consider:

- Make chores a team effort.
- Decide which chores each person is responsible for.
- Share less desirable chores.
- If there is a chore that you'd rather have completed a certain way, then you should do that task.
- Keep in mind, chores do not have to be equally divided.

Reactions

With serious thought, take the time to indicate how you might react, being honest with yourself, to the following circumstances.

1. You and your spouse are scheduled to work opposite shifts.
2. You discover that your spouse deals with jealousy.
3. Your spouse no longer has time for daily devotions.
4. A friend becomes flirtatious with your spouse.
5. You cannot get along with your sister-in-law.
6. You have a communication problem with your mother-in-law.
7. You have difficulty becoming pregnant.
8. Your apartment is too small, and you cannot afford a larger one.
9. Your spouse spends more money on himself/herself than on you.
10. You discover your spouse has incurred significant credit card debt.
11. Your spouse is laid off from his/her job.
12. Your sex life is less than exciting.
13. Communication becomes increasingly difficult.
14. You discover that your spouse cannot let go of his/her mother.
15. A job change requires you and your spouse to move to the other side of the country.

16. You find yourself battling an attraction to a coworker.
17. Your spouse's productivity and amount of time outside the home is greater than what is invested in the home.
18. Television and sports are far more important to your spouse than you ever realized.

Our Parents

Families of origin play a vital role when two persons are considering a lifetime together. Discuss your feelings about your parents and your future in-laws by answering the following questions.

1. Have you communicated to your parents your desire to be married? Yes _____ No _____

2. Are your father and mother in agreement with your plans for marriage? Yes _____ No _____

3. Do your parents agree with the length of your engagement and the date of the wedding? Yes _____ No _____

4. Have your parents expressed any hesitations concerning your desire to be married? Yes _____ No _____

5. Have your parents met his/her parents? Yes _____ No _____

6. Do you feel your parents are supportive of the person you want to marry? Yes _____ No _____

7. Are your parents Christians? Yes _____ No _____
    If not, how will that affect your relationship now or after you are married?

8. Will you attend your parents' church or another? Yes _____ No _____

9. Have you asked your parents for any wisdom or advice that they may have for you? Yes _____ No _____
    If so, what advice have they shared with you?

10. How can you maintain a spirit of honor toward your parents after you are married?

11. How often do you plan to visit your parents after you are married?

12. How will you respond to advice from your parents that you don't agree with?

13. Are there other matters concerning your parents or his/her parents that you have questions about?

14. I would like my marriage to be like my parents' marriage in the following ways:

15. I desire my marriage to differ from my parents' marriage in these ways:

Parent Questionnaire

(Permission is granted to photocopy this page.
One copy may be made for each parent.)

We believe that it is important to include parents as we help couples prepare for marriage. You have invested much love, time, energy, and finances into raising and training your child in order to see this point arrive in his/her life. Please respond in writing to the following questions and return them to your son or daughter so they may be shared in their next premarital counseling session.

1. Describe your relationship with your son or daughter:
   With your future son-in-law or daughter-in-law:

2. Express how you will help your child to "leave you" and "cleave" to his/her spouse.

3. Are you aware of any reasons that would prohibit this couple from marrying at this time?

4. How often do you expect to have visits with the newly married couple?

5. An area of adjustment that we foresee in our son's or daughter's marriage could be

6. Are you able to express a written word of blessing to this marriage? If yes, please expound below. If no, why not? Please explain.

_____

_____

_____

_____

_____

_____

_____

_____

_____

_____

_____

_____

_____

_____

_____

_____

_____

The following is an actual example of a written blessing:

Oh Carrie, the daughter of our youth, the apple of our eyes. From the day in Hawaii that we first knew you would join us, you have brought immeasurable joy to our lives. "Many daughters have done nobly, but you excel them all." Yes, Carrie, you have done nobly—you have chosen to revere the Lord, and for that you earn the praises of men. We bless you today, oh precious one. May you receive back the joy that you have given. While you will always be our precious daughter, in the days to come you will take on a new role—as wife...with all our love, all our support, all our hearts, we release you this day to be Jeremy's wife.

Jeremy Levi—we have prayed for you for over 24 years! Though we did not know your name, your smile, or your strength, we did know your character. For God called us to pray that *He* would raise up a son from a God-fearing home, a son obedient to His Word, a man to seek after *His* heart. So this day comes as no surprise...the only unknown was your name. And here you are—156 pounds of flesh and blood (and four pounds of ice cream and two pounds of chocolate!)—you're an answer to our prayers. Today we gladly, joyously receive you as a son. As you pledge to Carrie, we pledge to you both to support you and your marriage with all our hearts. Welcome, our son!

A Letter to My Parents

Compose a short letter of appreciation to your parents on a separate piece of paper in an effort to honor them (see Eph. 6:2-3). Following are areas you may want to consider:

- Giving you life
- Spiritual heritage
- Financial values
- Moral guidance
- Physical provision
- Encouragement
- Emotional support
- Education
- Athletic encouragement
- Discipline/training
- Love/affirmation/acceptance/approval
- Work ethic/skills
- Sacrifices/commitment

Please make a copy of this letter for yourself.

Are You Ready to Leave and Cleave?

Marriage predates Christianity. It goes back to Genesis, chapter 1. This study gives you both the opportunity to discover God's design for marriage. Review the Scriptures together and then with your premarital counselors.

1. Genesis 1:26-27

   The place to start. In the beginning God had a specific design in mind when He created humankind and instituted marriage. We were designed in His image, His likeness. He gave us dominion over the animals of the earth. God created both male and female.

2. Genesis 2:7,21-22

   Man was made from the dust of the earth, and God breathed the breath of life into him. Woman was created from the man. She was specifically designed to correspond to the man. Eve was "fashioned," while Adam was "formed."

3. Genesis 2:18

   Man's first need from God was a "helper suitable for him." God met the first problem that man encountered—loneliness. As Adam named the animals, he noticed that none of them were even close to being "suitable" or of his kind.

4. Genesis 2:23 and Ephesians 5:31

   Eve was given to Adam by God, and Adam said, "This is now bone of my bones and flesh of my flesh; she shall be called woman, for she was taken out of man." Eve was physically, spiritually, intellectually, emotionally, and relationally suitable for Adam. She was not like the animals. She was of the same flesh. A part of Adam's structure was used to fashion Eve.

   Man's strength is more external, while woman's strength is internal. A man desires to be noticed for what he accomplishes. A woman wants to be valued for who she is as a person. For Adam to be Adam, he needed Eve.

5. Genesis 2:24; Matthew 19:4-5; and Mark 10:6-8

   Before joining and cleaving, there needs to be a leaving. We leave father and mother to establish a new family unit. The focus becomes one another. Former friends, jobs, and extended family take on a lesser priority than this new union. This new household is under new authority. One man walks the bride up the wedding aisle (the father). Then another man (the new husband) walks her back down the aisle. As Dr. Ed Wheat writes, "Don't leave unless you plan to cleave."

6. Genesis 2:25 and Ephesians 5:31-32

Marriage means that two persons become one. Kevin is Sarah, and Sarah is Kevin. What affects Kevin affects Sarah. These two persons are now united. This union must be heterosexual and monogamous (see Prov. 5:15-23; 6:23-33).

There are three expressions of oneness in Scripture. These three expressions are (1) the Trinity (see 2 Cor. 13:14); (2) Christ and the Church (see Eph. 5:25-27; 31-32); and (3) marriage (see Gen. 2:24; Eph. 5:31).

The number one cannot be divided without the result being two halves. Separation and/or divorce is a separation of one person. This separation leaves two fractions of one.

From studying these Scriptures in the Book of Genesis, how do you perceive Adam and Eve being similar and yet completely different?

_____

_____

_____

_____

_____

_____

_____

_____

_____

_____

_____

_____

_____

_____

_____

_____

_____

_____

_____

Cooperative Mission

In Session One, you wrote about your individual mission or call from God. Genesis 1:28-30 and Genesis 2:15 reveal that Adam and Eve received instruction from God to be involved in a cooperative mission. God gave the garden, the earth, and the animals to Adam and Eve to care for together. When two become one, it is important not only to know our individual mission but also to understand our cooperative mission.

Take a moment with each other to write about how you see yourself involved after marriage in a cooperative mission with your future spouse. (For example: Brian is a vital part of the church worship team, and Megan teaches a Sunday school class for preschoolers. Those are individual missions. Together, Brian and Megan lead a home group for junior high students. That is a cooperative mission.)

_____

_____

_____

_____

_____

_____

_____

_____

_____

_____

_____

_____

_____

_____

_____

_____

_____

_____

_____

_____

Let's Talk

An effective communication system is vital to a stable, intimate, and satisfying marriage relationship. A breakdown of communication is almost always a primary cause of marital dysfunction. Ed Cole, author of *Communication, Sex, and Money*,[1] states that when communication stops, abnormality sets in, and the ultimate end of abnormality is death of the relationship. Just as faith dies when we refuse to communicate with our heavenly Father, so will a marriage die when a couple refuses to communicate. Ephesians 4:29-30 reveals that communication should edify, not corrupt. The Holy Spirit is grieved when we are not ministers of grace.

Our communication goals are to share with one another freely, to be lovingly honest about what we think and feel, to understand each other, to listen respectfully and respond appropriately, to be able to disagree and discuss our disagreements without becoming hurt or attacking one another, and to have conversation that is beneficial and uplifting. We will work toward these communication goals through various homework assignments including nonverbal communication, communication guidelines, effective communication, and scenario communication.

In *Training Christians to Counsel*,[2] Norm Wright, a well-known marriage counselor, states that communication can be broken down as follows:

7 percent words (content).

38 percent attitude (tone of voice).

55 percent body language.

Take this opportunity to begin to analyze your personal communication tendencies. What body language do you display when you are angry, hurt, or selfish? Under what circumstances does your tone of voice change? Even if you feel communication is one of your strong points, give full attention to the assignments which follow. Scripture has a lot to say about the way we talk to one another. Be open to discovering some hindrances to good communication that may be present in your life.

Nonverbal Communication

1. List at least five ways in which you have experienced nonverbal communication from each other (both positive and negative).

    1.
    2.
    3.
    4.
    5.

2. Share several experiences you have had concerning attitude and tone of voice while communicating with each other. (Again, share at least one positive and one negative experience.)

    1.
    2.

3. Identify any factors that have hindered communication (for example, in-laws, past relationships, beliefs, etc.).

    1.
    2.
    3.
    4.
    5.

4. Study the following verses and record what they reveal to you concerning nonverbal communication.

    Genesis 3:7-10 _____

    Genesis 4:5-6 _____

    Genesis 40:6-7 _____

    Joshua 7:6 _____

    1 Samuel 18:3-4 _____

    1 Kings 19:3-4 _____

    1 Kings 21:4 _____

    Proverbs 31:12-27 _____

    Mark 2:3-5 _____

    Luke 18:10-13 _____

    1 John 3:17-18 _____

How Do We Talk Together?

What kind of interaction do you have with each other? Respond to the following statements by placing a check at the answer that best describes him/her.

	Always	Usually	Sometimes	Rarely	Never
1. I listen to him/her.					
2. He/she listens to me.					
3. I understand what he/she is trying to say.					
4. He/she understands what I am trying to say.					
5. I show appreciation when he/she does things for me.					
6. He/she shows appreciation when I do things for him/her.					
7. I show interest in his/her ideas, thoughts, feelings, and activities.					
8. He/she shows interest in my ideas, thoughts, feelings, and activities.					
9. I feel comfortable disagreeing with what he/she says.					
10. I feel comfortable when he/she disagrees with me.					
11. I show interest in facts and information.					
12. He/she shows interest in facts and information.					
13. I am able to express feelings and emotions.					
14. He/she is able to express feelings and emotions.					
15. I am happy just to share and spend time with him/her.					
16. He/she is happy just to share and spend time with me.					
17. I am interested in his/her hobbies.					
18. He/she is interested in my hobbies.					
19. I respond in a thoughtful, non-judgmental way to him/her.					
20. He/she responds in a thoughtful, non-judgmental way to me.					

Communication Guidelines[3]

Think about the following guidelines and study the supporting Scriptures. You may complete the assignment individually or together.

Part A

1. Be a ready listener, and do not answer until the other person has finished talking (see Prov. 18:13; James 1:19).

2. Be slow to speak. Think first. Don't be hasty in your words. Speak in such a way that the other person can understand and accept what you say (see Prov. 15:23; 18:2; 29:20).

3. Don't go to bed angry! Each day, clear the offenses of that day. Speak the truth, but do it in love. Do not exaggerate (see Eph. 4:15,25-26).

4. Do not use silence to frustrate the other person. Explain why you are hesitant to talk at this time (see Prov. 15:28; 16:23). Plan a future time to finish the discussion.

5. Do not become involved in heated disputes. It is possible to disagree without attacking (see Prov. 17:14; 20:3; Eph. 4:31).

6. Do not respond in uncontrolled anger. Use a kind response and a soft tone of voice (see Prov. 14:29; 15:1; 25:15; 29:11).

7. When you are wrong, admit it, ask for forgiveness, and then ask how you can change (see Prov. 12:15; 16:2; 21:2; Matt. 5:23-25).

8. When someone confesses a wrong to you, tell that person you forgive him/her. Be sure it is forgiven and not brought up again to that person, to others, or to yourself (see Luke 17:3-4; Eph. 4:32; Col. 3:13).

9. Avoid nagging (Prov. 10:19; 21:19; 27:15).

10. Do not blame or criticize the other person. Instead, restore, encourage, and edify (Rom. 14:13; Gal. 6:1; 1 Thess. 5:11).

11. If someone verbally attacks, criticizes, or blames you, do not respond in the same manner (Rom. 12:17,21; 1 Peter 2:23; 3:9).

12. Try to understand the other person's opinion. Make allowances for differences (Eph. 4:2; Phil. 2:1-3).

13. Be concerned about the other person's interests (Phil. 2:4).

14. Do not gossip (Prov. 17:9; 18:8; 20:19; 26:22).

Part B

1. What attitudes or messages do the following sentences convey to you? Do they convey respect, appreciation, consideration, encouragement, affection, and love—or disdain, disrespect, rudeness, animosity, hostility, and rejection? Try to imagine someone saying these sentences to you.

"You don't really care."

"I really need you."

"Well, what do you have to complain about today?"

"It sounds like you had a difficult day. Is there any way I can help you?"

"You shouldn't feel that way!"

"I'm really sorry that you feel that way. How can I help? I'll be glad to pray for you and do anything I can."

"You never kiss me."

"Do you know what, honey? I really love you and like to have you hold me and kiss me."

"Well, what do you know? Miracles still happen. You're ready on time."

"Hey, hon, I just wanted you to know that I really appreciated that you were ready to go on time."

"Honey, you're terrific, and getting better all the time."

"You always forget what I ask you to do."

"I like the way you smile. It really brightens my day."

"We ought to have company more often. It's the only time we get good food around here."

"That was a super meal. You're a fantastic cook."

"How come you could get home early tonight when you can't other nights?"

"Boy, it's really great you got home early. I miss you during the day."

"I can't believe there's no money in the checking account. What did you spend it on?"

"Maybe there's a better way to discuss financial matters. Could we get some help?"

How to Become an Effective Communicator

Part A. The following Scriptures discuss interferences to healthy communication. As you study them, record the interferences in the blank provided. Number one has been completed as an example.

1. Ephesians 4:25 *Stop lying and speak the truth*
2. Ephesians 4:29 _____
3. Ephesians 4:31 _____
4. Colossians 3:8 _____
5. Colossians 3:9 _____
6. James 1:19 _____
7. Proverbs 11:13 _____
8. Proverbs 12:16 _____
9. Proverbs 12:18 _____
10. Proverbs 15:1 _____
11. Proverbs 15:5 _____
12. Proverbs 17:9 _____
13. Proverbs 18:2 _____
14. Proverbs 18:8 _____
15. Proverbs 18:13 _____
16. Proverbs 19:1 _____
17. Proverbs 19:5 _____
18. Proverbs 20:19 _____
19. Proverbs 25:24 _____
20. Proverbs 26:18-19 _____
21. Proverbs 26:20-21 _____
22. Proverbs 29:20 _____
23. Matthew 5:23-24 _____

Part B. From the list of Scriptures, what unhealthy patterns of communication can you identify in your life?

1. _____
2. _____
3. _____
4. _____
5. _____
6. _____
7. _____
8. _____
9. _____
10. _____

Part C. Below, list the steps you can take to begin changing these unhealthy patterns.

1. _____
2. _____
3. _____
4. _____
5. _____
6. _____
7. _____
8. _____
9. _____
10. _____

Have You Discussed...?

Have you both discussed...	Yes	No	Desire To
1. Any unmet expectations?	_____	_____	_____
2. Personality differences?	_____	_____	_____
3. Hurts you may have received from each other?	_____	_____	_____
4. The church you will attend when married?	_____	_____	_____
5. Who you will talk to after marriage concerning any unresolved problems?	_____	_____	_____
6. One another's families?	_____	_____	_____
7. Your most common self-criticisms?	_____	_____	_____
8. Things you have noticed concerning your relationship but are afraid to talk about?	_____	_____	_____
9. Jealousy you may have of one another?	_____	_____	_____
10. Topics upon which you disagree without losing your temper?	_____	_____	_____
11. How you will manage your money?	_____	_____	_____
12. Your parenting expectations?	_____	_____	_____
13. Your views regarding training children?	_____	_____	_____
14. Matters when one of you is quiet or sulking?	_____	_____	_____
15. Traditional versus nontraditional roles?	_____	_____	_____
16. Which one of you is more administrative?	_____	_____	_____
17. What family traditions you want to preserve?	_____	_____	_____
18. One another's cooking ability?	_____	_____	_____
19. One another's cleaning ability and expectations?	_____	_____	_____
20. Who will be the primary vehicle driver after marriage?	_____	_____	_____

When We Disagree

Disagreement is an opportunity for growth, both individually and as a couple. Disagreement affords us the privilege of listening and attempting to hear and understand another perspective. While that sounds nice, we know that at times it is difficult to follow through—especially in the heat of the moment. Disagreement does not need to be emotional. We sometimes become emotional out of a need to control life circumstances, especially when feeling insecure. At other times, in order to emphasize our point, or in an effort to preserve what dignity we think we may have left, our response may be filled with emotion.

Pride is that tool of human self-preservation which can be emotion-filled and eventually prove costly. The Bible tells us that a quiet answer turns away anger (see Prov. 15:1), but how then can you possibly win the disagreement? That depends on how you were trained to disagree. Was it loudly and with force or by simply walking away in fear? How would you like to be retrained to deal with those disappointing times of disagreement and anger? Admitting that you are upset is certainly a good first step. Admitting that you do not like losing a disagreement is powerful as well. Recognizing pride-filled defensive statements and mechanisms can be huge. Perhaps the most costly step of all is admitting that we might be wrong and having to initiate an apology. Apologizing to a stranger on the street may be a rather easy thing to do, but apologizing to someone you have invested your life into can be challenging. It means that you must humble yourself before the one you live with or work with. The closer the relationship, the more difficult an apology may be. Why? Our pride is at stake, and we desire to maintain it.

From the day we first accept Jesus into our lives, He begins to work in us. Jesus humbled Himself before man and became a servant (see Phil. 2:6-8). When we take on the nature of Christ, humble ourselves, and begin serving our mate, we know that the Father has been re-creating us to reflect His image. What else does the Scripture reveal? God gives grace to the humble (see Prov. 3:34). We are told to humble ourselves before the Lord (see James 4:10). With humility comes wisdom (see Prov. 11:2). And First Peter 5:5 reveals that we are to clothe ourselves with humility. In humility we are to consider others (our spouse) as better than ourselves (see Phil. 2:3).

What does this have to do with all the disagreements in which we find ourselves? If we are willing to put on the nature of Christ and humble ourselves, we will find our security in Him, not needing to come immediately to our own defense and attempt to preserve our personal pride. From our heart, we will desire to bring resolution to any disagreement in a way that honors the other and at the same time builds the relationship, rather than tearing it apart with unkind or belittling words. This person you are married to is you. If Steve and Mary are one, then Steve is Mary, and Mary is Steve. If one of us "wins" an argument, then we at the same time lose the argument because we are one.

You need your spouse's different opinion, different way of looking at things, his or her opposite view. That different view is to be embraced so together you can make a more informed decision and see the whole picture. While not all disagreements are connected to major life decisions, each one affords us the opportunity to humble ourselves, show grace, and establish our heart toward the will of the Father in the matter. We show value and honor to our mate when we listen to them. Desiring to understand their view says, "What you say is important, even if I don't agree."

Complete the following questions individually:

1. When a disagreement arises, I tend to:
   a. win at all costs.
   b. get quiet.
   c. look for the first exit.
   d. get stubborn and stand my ground.
   e. other

2. I knew my parents were in a conflict or disagreement because their tendency was to

3. When it comes to disagreements, I've been told by others that I have a tendency to

4. How I would prefer to deal with disagreements is to

5. When my fiancé/ée and I disagree we usually

6. Humbling myself is difficult because

7. What is the difference between a "quiet answer that turns away anger" and a "doormat" type of response?

8. Do you agree with the statement, "Disagreement is an opportunity for growth"? Why or why not?

9. How have you identified pride in your life when you are involved in a disagreement?

10. How would you like to handle disagreements when you are married?

Scenario Communication

Please indicate how you will respond to the following situations.

1. You have just arrived home from work. You are recounting an important conversation with your boss. Right in the middle of it your spouse asks, "Did you bring in the mail?"

2. You are mowing the yard. Your spouse asks you to go to the store for some milk, but you really want to finish mowing.

3. It has been over a week since the clothes were washed. You are out of socks.

4. You have had another heated discussion about your finances. Your spouse has purchased a non-budgeted item again.

5. You notice that whenever you have something important or confrontational to discuss with your spouse, he or she yawns and seems disinterested.

6. It seems that your spouse has difficulty picking up and putting away his or her things. You're wondering if he or she notices the items left on the floor.

Fighting Fair

Yes, this is a premarital issue, though *fighting* may seem like a strong word. Relationship is one of the best—and most challenging—gifts in life. Before you say "I do," we thought it would be appropriate to give to you an outline for fair fighting. In marriage oneness, if one spouse loses a fight, then you both lose. If one spouse wins, then you both win. Better decisions are made with input from both of you. When conflict arises, the following steps will guide you through a mature process of conflict resolution. Although similar to the previous section, the concepts are worth another read. Suggestion: Think of a recent discussion you and your finance may have had in which there were differences of opinion. Use these seven steps to walk through those differences.

1. **Understand/Identify**

   Understand that any two individuals will, from time to time, come into conflict. Understanding means listening and not just wanting to be understood. Identify what the conflict is, and then identify each person's understanding of the problem, as well as the feelings generated from this conflict.

2. **Set Aside Time**

   Set aside time to deal with the conflict. When emotions are out of control, take time to step back, calm down, think, and then come back together. (The use of a key phrase that signals we will come back together within a specified period of time to deal with the problem can be advantageous at this point. For example, "We need a cup of coffee.")

3. **Agreement**
    Discover the areas in which you agree—as well as the areas in which you do not.

4. **Stay on the Subject at Hand**
    Stay on the subject which represents the immediate conflict. Do not allow the conflict to wander off into other unrelated areas.

5. **Appreciate**
    Appreciate your spouse's opinion and what he or she adds to the process. When you value the ideas and feelings of your partner, you value that person.

6. **Identify the Needs**
    Allow for the needs of each partner to be met. When needs are met, conflict can be resolved. Identify the needs each of you has which are not being met in the conflict.

7. **Explore the Options and Move Toward a Solution**
    Explore options of resolution and move toward a solution. Prayer is a vital part of exploring the options and moving toward a solution. Take the time not only to listen to each other, but also to the Lord.

When a conflict or problem has been satisfactorily resolved, **close the issue.** This is very important. It is an active sign that you have made a decision you can both accept and that you are ready to move on. Move on. No reminders. Trust is the fruit that can follow.

Praying Together

Couple prayer is the most vital ingredient to a committed Christian marriage. The most intimate thing a couple can do together is to pray. Prayer is far more intimate than sex. When we pray with our mates, we discover their hearts; we discover their most intimate needs and desires.

Mary and I have always prayed together throughout our marriage. However, it wasn't until our sons entered public high school that we became desperately serious about petitioning the Father together on a daily basis. We realized that providing a prayer covering for our children was the most important thing we could do for them. Because prayer is so intimate, couples who are engaged should limit their prayer time, as well as being conscious about where they pray together. Praying in a dark room or sitting on a couch could lead to sensual closeness.

We believe that the enemy, making your most spiritual times together a temptation to be sensual, can confuse spirituality and sensuality. Be conscious of this fact.

Agreeing together in prayer (see Amos 3:3; Matt. 18:19) is far more powerful than arguing together. Listen to Art Hunt's words in his book, *Praying With the One You Love*: "Praying with your spouse is perhaps the most intimate thing you can do together. Think of what happens when you pray. There you are, right in front of God—and He can see right through you! And there by your side is your partner. You are both literally 'unveiled' before God. You may have already said, 'I trust you' to your spouse, but—this mutual prayer—is where the real risk comes into play...the bigger the risk, the bigger the reward. And in this case, the reward is enormous!"[4]

Some couples do not pray together because of vulnerability (it's risking too much); others avoid prayer because of feeling inadequate; some use the excuse that they do not have enough time; others simply do not trust their spouse enough. Whatever the reason, all of these reasons keep us from obedience to God, from growing together spiritually, from becoming passionately intimate, and from agreement that brings the deepest unity any two persons can encounter.

Perhaps you've already begun praying together. If not, we encourage you to begin now. If you establish this life-giving habit now, it will flow into your marriage relationship quite naturally.

Work through the following exercise together:

1. When is the best time for us to pray together?
2. Are there places we should avoid when praying together?
3. How can prayer lead to sensuality?
4. Before marriage, how much time should we spend praying together?
5. After marriage, our goal for prayer would be (how frequent and how long)...
6. Areas to cover in prayer before marriage might include:
7. Areas to cover in prayer after marriage can extend these and also include:
8. How can we avoid the temptation of busyness and keep prayer together a priority?

Endnotes

1. Edwin L. Cole, *Communication, Sex, and Money* (Southlake, TX: Watercolor Books, 2002).

2. H. Norman Wright, *Training Christians to Counsel* (Eugene, OR: Harvest House, 1977).

3. Adapted from Wayne Mack's *A Homework Manual for Biblical Counseling,* *vol. 1* (Phillipsburg, NJ: Presbyterian and Reformed Pub., 1979).

4. Art Hunt, *Praying With the One You Love* (Sisters, OR: Multnomah, 1996), 29.

Finances

Agreement is basic in successful marriages. "Can two walk together, unless they are agreed?" (Amos 3:3 NKJV). Financial agreement is an important marital goal. When partners agree concerning getting out of debt, tithing, overcoming a financial crisis, or being better stewards, then the power of God is released to work in their lives.

God's Word offers clear guidelines and principles for handling money. A scriptural overview of finances is included in this session. You will also have opportunity to express your personal financial views, to describe your financial background, to discover scriptural truths about finances together, and to work on a budget profile.

God wants you to have a strategy for financial health. Discover a place of agreement, and you will discover a place of blessing and provision.

Personal Financial Views

In order to discover and provide clarification regarding your personal financial views, answer the following questions without the help of each other.

1. Will you have joint or separate checking accounts?
   Will you participate in online banking? Yes _____ No _____
2. Who will do the bookkeeping?
3. Who will write the checks when paying bills?
4. Will you buy or rent a home? Buy _____ Rent _____
   If renting, how soon do you expect to buy?
5. How often will you go out to dinner?
6. Will you maintain a monthly budget? Yes _____ No _____
7. Will you use credit cards or borrow money?
8. When you use credit cards will you carry over a balance at the end of the month? Yes _____ No _____
9. Will you buy a car with borrowed money? Yes _____ No _____

10. What percentage of your paycheck should be saved each month?
11. What percentage of your income should be tithed?
12. Will you give offerings? Yes _____ No _____
13. Will the wife return to work after having children? Yes ____ No _____
14. What insurance(s) will you purchase?
15. Who will be responsible to make out a will?
16. How much freedom would you like to have when purchasing items without your spouse's approval?
17. How much spending money will you and your spouse normally have in your possession?
18. Will you carry personal debt into the marriage?
19. When do you plan to begin a retirement account?
20. Will you make use of automated paycheck or checking account debits when paying monthly expenses? Yes _____ No _____

Financial Background

Given the assumption that your parents' views toward money will have a profound effect on your views, discuss what you have observed about your parents' finances. Be prepared to share how your views are similar to or different from your parents' views of money.

1. Did your parents maintain a budget? Yes _____ No _____
2. Who was in charge of the finances?
3. Were the bills paid on time? Yes _____ No _____
4. Were your parents generous with those in need? Yes ___ No ___
5. Did your parents agree or did they argue a lot concerning money? _____
6. Did they focus on the necessities or did they purchase a lot of luxuries?
7. Did they take family vacations? Yes _____ No _____
8. Did one or both parents have a spending allowance?
9. Did your parents place importance on saving their money? Yes _____ No _____
10. Did your parents tithe or support mission work? Yes _____ No _____
11. How often did your family go out to eat?
12. How have your personal financial values been influenced by the financial values held by your parents?
13. If I could say one thing about my personal historical view of money, I would say
14. How has my view of finances changed since I have considered marriage?

Scriptural Truths About Finances

A.   Read the following Scriptures together and paraphrase the principles that you derive from each passage.
1.   Deuteronomy 8:17-18
2.   Proverbs 11:24-25
3.   Proverbs 11:28
4.   Proverbs 13:22
5.   Proverbs 22:1,4,7
6.   Ecclesiastes 5:10
7.   Jeremiah 9:23-24
8.   Matthew 6:19-21
9.   Luke 12:13-21
10. Romans 13:6-8
11. 1 Timothy 6:3-10,17-18
12. Hebrews 13:5

B.   Of the scriptural truths about finances listed above, share any areas that are of specific concern to you personally or that you believe need to be addressed with each other.

_____

_____

_____

_____

C.   How have these scriptural principles about finances challenged your personal view of money?

_____

_____

_____

_____

D.   Take a few minutes to read the following passage: Luke 16:10-12. Write about the connection Jesus makes between "worldly wealth" and "true riches."

The Personal Finances Budget

When two people come together in marriage, an entirely new financial picture is created; two incomes merge into one. This presents potential conflict if the couple does not follow practical guidelines for managing money.

Because budgeting is a lifelong exercise, the figures you record on your "Personal Finances Budget Sheet" will change over time—perhaps year to year. The budget sheet is simply a snapshot of income and expenses. But this snapshot can be amazingly eye-opening and life-changing. How we utilize our resources as stewards reveals a lot about us and our personal values when it comes to money.

As you plan your proposed budget together, use this budget sheet as a blueprint for your money management. Listing your assets and liabilities is good record keeping, and it will enable you and your counselors to "see" your spending plan, which in turn will help you to control your expenditures effectively.

Make several copies of the budget worksheet or use it as an example to create a spreadsheet on your computer.

Your finished product will help you establish financial goals and set priorities. We encourage you to not be overwhelmed with the process, but to embrace and enjoy the enlightening information you receive. If necessary, enlist the help and guidance of your premarital counselors to complete the budget sheet in its entirety.

Instructions

Together, record the known or estimated monthly dollar figure for each category on the budget sheet. (We've included two blank sheets for you.) The definitions of the categories are listed below to help you determine the scope of each one. The completed example will serve as a guideline.

Tithe: List your regular support (tithe) to your church. (Anything over 10 percent may be listed under the *Giving* category.)

Tax: List federal, state, and county taxes.

Investment: List any money invested for future care of your family (IRAs, retirement programs, home savings, etc.).

Mortgage/Rent: List mortgage payment or rent payment.

Maintenance: If you own your home, estimate monthly maintenance costs.

Utilities: List your monthly utility costs: electricity, heat, water, sewer, trash.

Telephone/Internet: Estimate your monthly phone bills including cell phones, as well as cable and Internet costs.

Food & Supplies: Include food (work and school lunches), drugstore supplies, department store sundries (toiletries, laundry).

Clothing: Estimate a monthly budget.

Auto Payment/Lease: List auto payment(s) and the cost of insurance, driver's licenses, vehicle registration, gas, and maintenance.

Medical/Dental: Include money spent for medicines, and medical, dental, optical appointments.

Gifts: List monthly expenses for gifts (birthdays, weddings, Christmas, graduations, etc.).

Dining: List restaurant meals.

Travel/Vacation: List weekend travel and yearly vacations.

Recreation/Entertainment: List money spent for family activities and sporting events (swimming, bowling, movies, football games, etc.).

Miscellaneous: List expenses not covered above: college loans, marriage seminars, magazine subscriptions, and postage.

Personal Debt: List credit card bills and any other loans.

Giving: List missionary support and special offerings.

Savings: List money set aside for emergencies. Indicate withdrawals with brackets [ ].

When the monthly budget amounts are completed, compute the totals. First, work from left to right, adding annual totals for each category. The annual totals added together, excluding income, can be more than, equal to, or less than the total annual income. Figure the average monthly total for each category by dividing each annual total by 12.

If you discover a specific area of your budget sheet to be higher than you anticipated (for example, the miscellaneous category), try recording all of your expenditures in that category for one month. You may be surprised at the total when you keep record of every pack of gum or cup of coffee you purchase randomly.

Personal Finances Budget Sheet

Category	Jan	Feb	Mar	April	May	June	July	August	Sept	Oct	Nov	Dec	Amount Total	Average Total
Income: Husband	2250	2250	2812	2250	2250	2813	2250	2250	2812	2250	2250	2813	29250	2438
Wife	825	825	1031	825	825	1031	825	825	1031	825	825	1031	10725	894
Tithe	308	307	384	307	308	384	308	307	384	307	308	384	3996	333
Federal Tax	520	520	649	520	520	650	520	520	649	520	520	650	3758	563
State Tax	93	93	116	63	63	116	63	63	116	63	63	116	1208	100
County Tax	31	31	38	31	31	38	31	31	38	31	31	38	400	33
Investment / FICA	246	246	307	246	246	307	246	246	307	246	246	307	3196	267
Mortgage	0	0	0	0	0	0	0	0	0	0	0	0	0	0
Rent	550	550	550	550	550	550	550	550	550	550	550	550	660	550
Maintenance	0	0	0	0	0	0	0	0	0	0	0	0	0	0
Electricity	95	95	95	95	95	95	95	95	95	95	95	95	1140	65
Heat	0	0	0	0	0	0	0	0	0	0	0	0	0	0
Water	0	0	0	0	0	0	0	0	0	0	0	0	0	0
Sewer	0	0	0	0	0	0	0	0	0	0	0	0	0	0
Trash	0	0	0	0	0	0	0	0	0	0	0	0	0	0
Telephone / Internet	100	100	100	100	100	100	100	100	100	100	100	100	1200	100
Food & Supplies	350	350	350	350	350	350	350	350	350	350	350	350	4200	350
Clothing	75	75	75	75	75	75	75	75	75	75	75	75	900	75
Auto Payment / Lease	0	0	0	0	0	0	0	0	0	0	0	0	0	0
Auto Gas	125	125	125	125	125	125	125	125	125	125	125	125	1500	125
Auto Insurance	0	0	750	0	0	0	0	0	750	0	0	0	1500	125
Auto License / Reg.	0	0	0	36	0	0	0	0	0	0	0	0	36	3
Auto Maintenance	75	75	75	75	75	75	75	75	75	75	75	75	900	75
Medical / Dental	80	80	80	80	80	80	80	80	80	80	80	80	960	80
Gifts	40	40	40	40	40	40	40	40	40	40	40	40	480	40
Dining	0	0	0	60	0	0	60	0	0	60	0	0	180	15
Travel / Vacation	0	0	0	0	0	0	300	400	0	0	0	0	700	58
Rec / Entertainment	30	30	30	30	30	30	30	30	30	30	30	30	360	30
Education	0	0	175	0	0	0	0	175	0	0	0	175	525	44
Subscriptions	0	36	0	0	0	0	0	0	0	0	0	0	36	3
Health / Life Insurance	50	50	50	50	50	50	50	50	50	50	50	50	600	50
Debt	0	0	0	0	0	0	0	0	0	0	0	0	0	0
Miscellaneous	125	125	125	125	125	125	125	125	125	125	125	125	1500	125
Giving	50	50	50	50	50	50	50	50	50	50	50	50	500	50
Savings	133	97	[321]	37	132	604	[228]	[442]	[146]	73	132	429	500	42
Cumulative Savings	133	230	[91]	[54]	78	682	454	12	[134]	[61]	71	500		

Personal Finances Budget Sheet

Category	Jan	Feb	Mar	April	May	June	July	August	Sept	Oct	Nov	Dec	Amount Total	Average Total
Income: Husband														
Wife														
Tithe														
Federal Tax														
State Tax														
County Tax														
Investment / FICA														
Mortgage														
Rent														
Maintenance														
Electricity														
Heat														
Water														
Sewer														
Trash														
Telephone / Internet														
Food & Supplies														
Clothing														
Auto Payment / Lease														
Auto Gas														
Auto Insurance														
Auto License / Reg.														
Auto Maintenance														
Medical / Dental														
Gifts														
Dining														
Travel / Vacation														
Rec / Entertainment														
Education														
Subscriptions														
Health / Life Insurance														
Debt														
Miscellaneous														
Giving														
Savings														
Cumulative Savings														

Sexual Relations

God is the creator of sex. He originated lovemaking between married partners. Sex is "a beautiful and intimate relationship shared uniquely by a husband and wife," write Tim and Beverly LaHaye in their book *The Act of Marriage.*[1]

In His Word, God has given much information and many directions about sexual relations. He does not consider sex an embarrassing topic. He addresses marriage in a discreet and wholesome way.

God wants you to go into marriage informed about and prepared for sexual relations. God's desire is that you anticipate and then enjoy this wonderful aspect of the marriage relationship. Videos, books, and audio tapes on the subject of sexual relations are available to the Church today and are authored by knowledgeable and dedicated Christians. Take advantage of these resources to help you understand God's intent for sexual relations.

Exercises in this session will provide a scriptural look at sex in marriage, questions for discussion, an examination of personal attitudes and beliefs, sexual anatomy identification, and some practical information that will help you to become a caring and creative lover.

Finally, you will find helpful information about birth control in appendix C and honeymoon precautions in appendix D. Answers to the matching questions, the anatomy diagram, and the true or false statements are found in appendix E.

Sex in Marriage

A Look at the Scriptures

Express briefly, in your own words, what each of the following Scriptures reveals concerning attitude, reproduction, communication, and sexual pleasure within the boundaries of marriage.

Genesis 2:24-25—What will leaving parents and being united to our spouse bring forth?   Song of Solomon 4:1-12; Proverbs 5:15-21; 1 Corinthians 7:2-5—How is sexual pleasure part of God's purpose for marriage?

Genesis 1:28; Deuteronomy 7:13-14; Psalm 127:3-5; 139:13-15—What is the blessing that physical oneness can produce between a husband and wife?

Hebrews 13:4; 1 Corinthians 6:12—Are there any limitations on sexual pleasure for a married couple?

Have you had any past sexual experiences that you now know would violate God's scriptural boundaries? If "yes," please explain. _____
_____ Do you feel any guilt or sexual shame? How will you not carry this into your marriage?

Questions for Discussion

Answer the following questions to the best of your ability according to your perceptions, without each other's help. Use an additional sheet of paper if necessary.

1. Do you feel that being Christians will make any difference in your sexual relationship?

2. Will you be able to discuss with your spouse what you do not know about sexual relations?

3. What worries you or preoccupies you concerning your sexual relationship?

4. After marriage, how do you expect to communicate your desire to have sexual intercourse?

5. Are there any memories of the past that would have a negative effect on your present attitude or feelings concerning your sexual relationship within marriage?

6. Can you recall the source from which you first heard about sexual reproduction? If so, explain.

7. Were you free to ask your parents questions about sex? What was their response?

8. Can you remember any specific attitudes or expressions of your parents concerning sexual relations?

9. Is it possible for marriage partners to be involved in lust toward one another?

10. Is there anything that embarrasses you concerning sexual relations?

11. How often do you expect to engage in sexual relations each month with your spouse?

12. Do you have any apprehension concerning sex within marriage? If so, explain.

13. What purpose, if any, would masturbation (self-stimulation) serve within a marriage?

14. What type(s) of contraceptives are you considering? Do you agree on birth control? Who will be responsible for birth control? Have you consulted your physician?

15. Have the two of you discussed your desires to have children, including how soon, how many, and how close?

A Creative Plan

Even though a creative plan cannot be implemented until after you say "I do," read and discuss these eight characteristics together with your premarital counselors. By being open and honest now, you can overcome inhibitions in becoming a creative lover.

I. **Sexual Pleasure Is God's Idea**
    A.   Sexual pleasure is God's intent for marriage. Procreation is not the only purpose for sex.
    B.   Sexual fulfillment is a process. It is a learned experience.
        1.   Know God's intent (review the "Sex in Marriage" exercise).
        2.   God's desire is to encourage you and liberate you sexually.
    C.   Open and honest communication about the sexual relationship is necessary.
        1.   Clearly communicate what is enjoyable to you.
        2.   Ask what is enjoyable to your spouse.

II. **Eight Characteristics of a Creative Lover**
    A.   Be totally available (see 1 Cor. 7:3-5).
        1.   Do not deprive your husband or wife except for prayer and fasting.
        2.   Schedule nights for time together. Take a nap if necessary.
        3.   If you find yourself lacking sexual desire, know that right action will generate desire. If this lack of desire remains for an extended period of time, consult your physician.
        4.   What is at stake when you say no? Feelings of rejection can develop.
    Note: You can be a very loving wife or husband, but if you consistently turn your spouse down sexually, the other things you do will be negated.
    B.   Be carefree.
        1.   Know that sexual response for a woman is tied to her emotions.
        2.   Put your cares aside and freely give yourself to one another.
        3.   If there is a lot on your mind, pray, then give each other a backrub.
        4.   If there is hurt between you, work it out before lovemaking.
    C.   Be attractive. Appearance affects our attraction to each other.
        1.   Always do your best to be presentable, attractive to your spouse.
        2.   Don't always look "grubby" at home.

3. Take care of yourself (shower, shave, makeup, etc.) even if you aren't going out.

4. Wear attractive underwear. Wear attractive nightwear. Use cologne and perfume.

D. Be eager. Anticipate sexual experiences with one another.

1. Fantasize about one another.

2. Let God liberate you to daydream about your physical time together (see Song of Solomon chapters 4 and 8).

3. Practice thinking about your husband or wife. Think positive things about your physical relationship (see Phil. 4:8).

E. Be creative. Study your spouse. Find out what excites him or her. What turns him or her on? Pursue creative avenues to ignite these desires.

1. Do things differently. Be romantic.

2. Do not try to meet your spouse's need with what you like.

3. Do not worry about other marriages. Study your own.

F. Be interested. Do not let lovemaking become predictable and boring.

1. You do not serve the same frozen TV dinner every night, do you? Sex will lose its interest if you are not involved in doing things differently. Communicate about this.

2. Are you willing to make love at unorthodox times? Are you willing to try new places? Are you willing to try new things?

G. Be uninhibited (see Gen. 2:25).

1. Adam and Eve were naked and were not ashamed. They were totally free to give themselves without inhibitions.

2. Accept yourself—your spouse chose *you*!

3. Do not get hung up on imperfections.

4. Do the things that you can do. Come to terms with how you look. Don't compare yourself.

5. Communicate with your spouse the area(s) you want to change (losing weight, gaining weight, cutting your hair, etc.).

H. Be aggressive. This advice is especially for the woman, because the man usually takes the initiative.

1. Totally give yourself—be excited, be thrilled.

2. Don't be boring and passive. Sexual relations are not just to meet biological needs.

3. Allow God to liberate you in responsiveness with consideration of your partner's feelings. Men should read First Peter 3:7.

III. **Be Involved.** Follow these eight steps after marriage, and your sexual lives will blossom. Don't settle for second best. Decide to pursue God's desire of sexual pleasure in marriage.
   A. Men are turned on by sight (undressing).
   B. Women are turned on emotionally and by physical contact (light touching).
   C. A woman is like an iron (she heats up slowly).
   D. A man is like a light bulb (he turns on instantly).
   E. Foreplay must be gentle and not rushed. Foreplay for the woman must begin before the bedroom.
   F. Lovemaking takes time. There may be times when we meet biological needs only, but this is *not* the norm.
   G. Use proper language.
   H. Be clean, brush your teeth, shave, and so forth.

IV. **Sexual Oneness**—for true sexual oneness, our motive must be unselfish love toward our mate and our means must be grace. We minister to one another through unselfish, unconditional love that gives regardless of what the recipient may deserve (grace). Through time as a husband or wife, you will grow in your own understanding of your sexual responses. Communicate with each other what you have discovered so that your sexual pleasure continues to grow and is fulfilling to both of you.

V. **An Important Note**—Please keep in mind that any form of pornographic material is not healthy for you or your marital oneness. Pornography is false intimacy, and it is addictive. Once one indulges, there is an insatiable desire for more. Never bring it into your marriage. It does not help sexual oneness; pornography actually hinders sexual oneness. It devalues your mate and what God has given you.

If you are involved with any form of pornography, stop. If you feel that you are unable to stop, seek pastoral and professional help immediately. Take this sin to your heavenly Father; repent and ask Him for His solution.

Attitudes and Beliefs About Sex

On your own, place an *A* for Agree or a *D* for Disagree before each statement below.

_____ 1. It is not the woman's responsibility to initiate sexual relations.

_____ 2. Sexual response can diminish when tension exists in the marriage.

_____ 3. Sex should never be a scheduled activity.

_____ 4. Sexual intimacy is important to a rewarding marriage relationship.

_____ 5. Mutual orgasm always occurs with sexual intercourse.

_____ 6. Present sexual dysfunction may be the result of past sexual abuse or misinformation.

_____ 7. Sex should never be used as a reward or punishment.

_____ 8. A couple should not hesitate to seek counseling when experiencing sexual difficulties.

_____ 9. Abstaining from sexual intimacy is permissible when one partner is fasting.

_____ 10. It is permissible to withhold or demand sex from your spouse.

_____ 11. It is God's purpose for sex to be desirable and satisfying to both partners.

_____ 12. Making excuses to avoid sexual relations is natural and should be expected.

_____ 13. A married couple should fully communicate to each other what pleases them sexually.

_____ 14. Because your body is not your own, you or your spouse can request or be involved in any kind of sexual behavior within your marriage.

Matching Questions
(Answers found in appendix E)

1. STD	A. period of greatest sexual excitement
2. ejaculation	B. absence of sexual desire
3. incest	C. the virus that causes AIDS
4. coitus	D. inability of male to perform sexual relations
5. impotence	E. external organs of reproduction
6. HIV	F. periodic discharge of uterine lining
7. copulation	G. refraining from sexual relations
8. erection	H. swelling, firmness of penis during sexual excitement
9. semen	I. surgical procedure which results in inability to conceive
10. heterosexual	J. sexual intercourse
11. frigidity	K. synonymous for climax
12. AIDS	L. sexually attracted to opposite sex
13. menstruation	M. reproductive cell of female
14. sperm	N. secretion discharged by male at time of orgasm
15. climax	O. venereal disease which causes sterility
16. ovum	P. coitus between those of near relationship
17. sterilization	Q. indulging in sexual relations with many partners
18. genitals	R. acquired immune deficiency syndrome
19. promiscuity	S. production and release of egg from ovary
20. orgasm	T. sexually transmitted disease
21. homosexual	U. having sexual attraction to persons of same sex
22. ovulation	V. engaging in sexual intercourse outside of marriage
23. fornication	W. male fluid of reproduction
24. masturbation	X. self-stimulation of genitals for sexual gratification
25. gonorrhea	Y. same as coitus
26. abstinence	Z. ejection of seminal fluids from the male urethra

Anatomy

How well do you know the proper names for male and female sex organs? The drawings on this page show one half of the human body divided in the center from front to back. Given the proper name, identify each part by its number on the diagram. In the blank spaces write each appropriate number (answers in appendix E).

Male

glans penis _____

penis _____

prostate gland _____

scrotum _____

seminal vesicles _____

testicle _____

urethra _____

vas deferens _____

Female

cervix _____

clitoris _____

Fallopian tube _____

labia _____

ovary _____

urethra _____

uterus or womb _____

vagina _____

True or False

With or without the help of each other, write *T* or *F* in the space provided before each of the following statements (answers in appendix E).

_____ 1. The typical menstrual cycle occurs every 28 days and lasts for 5-7 days.

_____ 2. The foreskin is partially removed in circumcision.

_____ 3. The ova are formed in the Fallopian tubes.

_____ 4. Pregnancy is most likely to occur at ovulation—14 days prior to the onset of menstruation.

_____ 5. The most common form of female contraception is the birth control pill.

_____ 6. Using a condom guarantees the AIDS virus cannot be transmitted from one partner to another.

_____ 7. When the Fallopian tubes are closed by disease or surgery, pregnancy cannot occur.

_____ 8. The birth control pill prevents ovulation from occurring.

_____ 9. The scrotum covers and protects the male organs that produce male reproductive cells.

_____ 10. Venereal disease can be acquired through contact with toilet seats.

_____ 11. A monogamous relationship is the best prevention of sexually transmitted diseases.

_____ 12. Herpes, genital warts, chlamydia, and HPV (human papilloma virus) are examples of STDs, which are increasing in incidence.

_____ 13. The AIDS virus is transmitted through semen, vaginal secretions, and blood.

_____ 14. Women infected with the AIDS virus may infect their unborn babies.

_____ 15. "Honeymoon cystitis" is a common bladder infection found in newly married virgins.

_____ 16. A missed period always indicates pregnancy.

_____ 17. The sperm and egg meet in the Fallopian tube.

_____ 18. Ovulation does not occur as long as a woman is nursing an infant.

_____ 19. The most sensitive sexual area of the female is the clitoris.

_____ 20. All women are negatively affected by PMS one week prior to menstruation.

Married Sex Is Better Sex

In the book *The Case for Marriage*,[2] authors Linda Waite and Maggie Gallagher write that married persons have better sex, and, in fact, have sex more frequently than do single persons. Among the married, sex can be enjoyed more—physically, emotionally, and spiritually. Married sex is better because

- Sex fits into their everyday lives due to their close proximity.
- There is a long-range commitment to invest in and please their spouse.
- Married persons are committed to monogamy.
- The married couple knows one another better—their likes and dislikes.
- Married sex is the only "safe sex" versus dangerous encounters full of excitement but followed by worry and anxiety.

List other reasons why you think sex within marriage is God's better idea.

1.
2.
3.

Sex Within Marriage Can Be Damaging as Well.

Sex should never be used as a means of control. It should never be demeaning or physically abusive. Never should there be any form of sex that would embarrass another or be against their will or conscience. Sex is never meant to inflict pain upon one's spouse. Sex is not about "me"; it's about the law of love which honors one's spouse above self. When sex is selfish, it is lust-filled rather than love-filled. Love is giving, and lust is taking. Love is satisfying while lust is insatiable. Sex is damaging if it is forced or coerced; it should never shame another. Sex is damaging when it is used as a replacement for affection and closeness. Sex is unhealthy when a personal sense of worth is sought through sex. Sex is unhealthy when it is used as punishment or for exercising power and control over another.

Are there any other damaging aspects of sex? Share those with your counselors and your fiancé/ée.

What Inhibits Sex in Marriage?

There are many areas of life that can inhibit our sexual responses. We have listed a few for you to discuss together.

1. Over-scheduling, self-depletion
2. Lack of communication
3. Not serving one another

4. Lack of non-sexual touch
5. Pornography
6. Not planning times of intimacy
7. Poor hygiene
8. Unresolved conflict
9. Lack of encouragement and affirmation
10. Lack of prayer and spiritual oneness

Are there other reasons that would inhibit intimacy within marriage? Share those areas with your fiancé/ée and your counselors.

In the Case of Sexual Abuse History

When someone has experienced a form of sexual abuse or molestation, there can be unique intimacy challenges presented within the marriage. It is never God's will for something destructive and demeaning to happen to any human being. He is not the author of such behavior, but He is the healer.

If you have had this type of experience, it is best to share it openly with an appropriate and experienced counselor who can help you. Such life experiences have a way of surfacing within marriage, creating intimacy issues. Being honest, seeking counsel, and exposing to the light what occurred in the dark, will promote healing in you and at the same time decrease the negative effects upon your union.

Healing is a process. As you grow in your understanding of the process that the Father moves you through, along with an abundant supply of patience and kindness from your mate, sexual intimacy can become your strength.

Endnotes

1. Tim and Beverly LaHaye, *The Act of Marriage* (Grand Rapids, MI: Zondervan, 1998).

2. Linda Waite and Maggie Gallagher, *The Case for Marriage: Why Married People Are Happier, Healthier, and Better Off Financially* (New York: Broadway Books, 2001).

Marriage Ceremony Planning

This is your special day. What kind of wedding ceremony do you want? To help you, we have included a sample ceremony at the end of this session. Embrace and enjoy each aspect of the planning—from choosing invitations, gowns, and flowers to writing your vows and making arrangements for the honeymoon.

Your counselors will offer helpful resources for planning your ceremony and writing your vows. This session includes exercises addressing your call together and what's in a vow. You will also find a study of what takes place in the spiritual realm during the wedding. Peruse these pages carefully together. Please direct any questions or comments to your counselors. You may also desire to discuss some of these points with your parents. You may have questions for your pastor or the one(s) responsible for marrying you at this time.

The final exercise in this chapter is a study on "submission." This exercise will bring an understanding of God's scriptural basis for government in marriage.

Do not allow yourselves to become anxious or frustrated with details. Bathe each decision in prayer. This is a one-time experience, and you will be grateful for happy memories. We want to remind you to schedule your wedding early in the day. It has taken a lot of preparation to arrive at this point. The wedding day will be a long one. The earlier you marry, the earlier you can leave for your first night of marriage; with an earlier ceremony, you will have energy left over for one another.

Called Together?

Once again, congratulations are in order. You have completed five or more sessions in preparation for your life together. Hopefully you now have a better understanding of the commitment you are about to make.

Perhaps you have come to the conclusion that you may not be ready for marriage. Even more painful than deciding not to get married at this point would be to spend your life feeling unsure if marriage was the right choice. If you have substantial reasons for not moving into marriage, do not ignore these convictions.

Maturely and honestly acknowledge these reasons to each other and your counselor. Seek counsel and be absolutely sure about your decision.

Many of you, however, as a result of completing this study course, have an increased desire to be married. Hopefully you have discovered how honesty and openness cause personal growth and enhance your relationship.

Work for unity in planning your wedding ceremony. This is your special day. Here are some questions to consider together when planning your wedding ceremony.

1. What do you want your wedding ceremony to reflect to the persons attending?

2. Share several ways in which you would like to communicate God's presence in your ceremony.

3. How do you want those who attend to participate in this celebration with you?

4. Will you write your own vows? Yes _____ No _____

5. Do you want the officiating minister to deliver a sermon?
   Yes _____ No _____
   If so, what would you like to have included in the message?
   _____

6. Is your wedding budget reasonable? Yes _____ No _____

7. Have you discussed this budget with your parents? Yes _____ No _____

8. Are your parents helping financially with the wedding?
   Yes ___ No ____

9. Are there ways you should honor your parents in the ceremony?
   Yes _____ No _____ If so, how?

10. Have your parents expressed special preferences for the ceremony that you do not wish to include?
    Yes _____ No _____ If so, how will you deal with this?

Finally, do not allow the excitement of this day to rob you of creating life-long memories. Most importantly, rejoice and be glad that two are being called together as one.

What's in a Vow?

"If a man makes a vow to the Lord, or swears an oath to bind himself by some agreement, he shall not break his word; he shall do according to all that proceeds out of his mouth" (Numbers 30:2).

Webster's defines *vow* as "a solemn promise or pledge that commits one to act or behave in a particular way."[1] That obligation, promise, or pledge would include your marriage vows. *Marriage,* according to Scripture, is a covenant to companionship. A covenant was the most binding contract in the Bible. It was an oath with great penalties if broken.

There should be no consideration given to the breaking of a marriage vow. The follower of Christ should not have a disagreement so large that it leads to divorce. Jesus said in Mark 10:9, "Therefore what God has joined together, let not man separate."

Your vows are spoken to one another, to God, and to those who witness your marriage ceremony. Do not take them lightly. Listen to what the Book of Ecclesiastes states concerning a vow: "When you make a vow to God, do not delay to pay it; for He has no pleasure in fools. Pay what you have vowed—better not to vow than to vow and not pay" (Eccles. 5:4-5).

What's in a vow? It's a commitment, a promise, a pledge, an obligation to remain married…"until death do us part."

Will you write your own vows? What words of commitment, value, promise, and pledge do you desire to include in your vows?

Saying I Do
What Happens at a Wedding

The marriage union gives birth to many radical changes. The least visible of these changes take place in the spiritual realm. The following is a study outline intended to point out some of those important changes. Thoroughly cover the following with each other and your premarital counselors.

I.   A Transfer of Authority
    A.   Prior to the wedding, the bride and the groom are under the authority of another.
        1.   The woman comes to the wedding with her father (with whom she has spent most of her life) and leaves with her husband (with whom she will spend the remainder of her life).
        2.   The man leaves father and mother to cleave to his wife.
    B.   After the wedding, the husband is commanded to be the authority for another, his wife.
        1.   This includes spiritual leadership, as well as the responsibility to care for and draw counsel from his wife.
    C.   The woman changes her name.
        1.   The father gives his daughter away.
        2.   The bride accepts a new name.

II. An Exchange of Possessions

    A.   The husband and wife no longer belong to themselves. They will give of themselves in three areas:

        1.   Their spirits—the most intimate area (where God dwells)

        2.   Their souls—the intellect, will, and emotions

        3.   Their bodies—the flesh (including the skills of the flesh)

    B.   They give away their possessions:

        1.   Automobiles, furniture, and so forth

        2.   Money

    C.   They give away their problems:

        1.   Physical

        2.   Financial

        3.   Relational

III. New Responsibility

    A.   "…The head of every man is Christ, the head of woman is man, and the head of Christ is God" (1 Corinthians 11:3).

        1.   A husband is responsible to Christ.

        2.   A wife is responsible to her husband.

        3.   Christ is responsible to God.

    B.   As the husband is submitted to Christ, so the wife is to be submitted to her husband, allowing him to be responsible for her.

    C.   Husbands love your wives (see Eph. 5:25-33; 1 Peter 3:7).

        1.   Giving himself

        2.   Honoring her, being considerate

        3.   Giving of his name

        4.   Caring for her

        5.   Leaving past relationships

        6.   Living for her (dying to himself)

        7.   Treating her with respect

IV. New Purposes

    A.   To give happiness (blessing) to another

        1.   Your happiness comes from making your spouse happy.

    B.   To bring fulfillment to your spouse in marriage

        1.   Make your spouse's life meaningful.

    C.   To experience the fullness of being complemented by another

V. Schedule Changes

    A.   Major changes take place in individual schedules, environments, or even geographical areas.

VI. Additional Relationships

A. Marriage into the spouse's family requires special love and grace.

B. Accept and reach out to meet the needs of the in-laws.

C. Involve yourself with the friends of your spouse, and accept friendships he/she has brought into the marriage.

D. Additional relationships will come after having children.

VII. Wider Interests

A. As you receive the abilities, interests, and areas of expertise of your spouse, they become increasingly beneficial to you.

B. As your spouse grows, rather than losing your identity, you become enriched by what your spouse adds to your relationship.

C. Interests should become mutually beneficial.

D. Each mate is a lifetime study; you continually study your mate to know him/her and to understand his/her needs.

E. Everything your mate is, knows, and is becoming is yours to share.

Sample Ceremony[2]

The following marriage ceremony schedule can help you begin planning your own special day. It includes the basic structure of a Christian wedding, as well as traditions found in many weddings. Ask the Holy Spirit to guide you as you creatively plan your marriage ceremony.

The Marriage Ceremony of
Mark Richard Windsor and Victoria Anne Chancery
February 14 at 11:00 A.M.

Prelude (10:40 A.M.)

"Together as One"

"Make Us One"

"Great Is the Lord"

    (Mark escorts his parents as the pastor, Henry, Tom, and Jeff enter from the side door.)

Processional (11:00 A.M.)

"Joyful, Joyful" (Bridesmaids enter)

"Bridal Chorus" (Victoria and her father enter)

Giving of the Bride Pastor

Pastor: "Who gives this bride in marriage?"

Father: "Her mother and I."

    (Mark steps forward. Mark and Victoria face the front.)

Prayer

Pastor "I ask that the congregation remain standing as we come before the Lord in prayer."

"The congregation may be seated."

Message (10-15 minutes)   Pastor

(Include charge of faith to couple and witnesses.)

Wives, submit to your own husbands, as to the Lord. For the husband is head of the wife, as also Christ is head of the church; and He is the Savior of the body. Therefore, just as the church is subject to Christ, so let the wives be to their own husbands in everything. Husbands, love your wives, just as Christ also loved the church and gave Himself for her, that He might sanctify and cleanse her with the washing of water by the word, that He might present to Himself a glorious church, not having spot or wrinkle or any such thing, but that she should be holy and without blemish. So husbands ought to love their own wives as their own bodies; he who loves his wife loves himself. For no one ever hated his own flesh, but nourishes and cherishes it, just as the Lord does the church. For we are members of His body, of His flesh and of His bones. "For this reason a man shall leave his father and mother and be joined to his wife, and the two shall become one flesh." This is a great mystery, but I speak concerning Christ and the church (Ephesians 5:22-32).

To Groom: "Have you received Jesus Christ as Lord and Savior of your life?"

Response: "I have."

To Bride: "Have you received Jesus Christ as Lord and Savior of your life?"

Response: "I have."

"The Bible tells us that any man who is in Christ is a new creation; old things have passed away and all things have become new. Mark and Victoria, your expression of faith makes you one with Jesus Christ!"

To You as Witnesses

"To the congregation, as well as to the world, I announce that Mark and Victoria stand before you cleansed by the shed blood of their personal Savior, Jesus."

"Jesus said in the eighteenth chapter of Matthew's Gospel, 'Again, I say to you, that if two of you agree on earth concerning anything that they will ask, it will be done for them by My Father in heaven'" (Matt. 18:19)

"You as a congregation are here to bear witness of this marriage. You are also here to stand before God in agreement with this union. Mark and Victoria desire your blessing upon their call together."

(Mark and Victoria move up onto platform.)

Profession of Vows   Pastor

To Groom: "Mark, do you take Victoria to be your wife, to be one with your flesh, to love her as Christ loves the church, to be faithful to her the remainder of your life?"

Response: "I do."

To Groom: "Please turn to Victoria and make this profession of your faith to her." (Hand card to Mark. He reads it.)

Groom: "I, Mark, take you, Victoria, to be my wife. I promise before God and these witnesses to be your loving and faithful husband, in plenty and in want, in joy and in sorrow, in adversity and in health, as long as we both shall live."

To Bride: "Victoria, do you take Mark to be your husband, to be one with his flesh, submitting yourself to him as unto the Lord, showing reverence to him as the head of this union for the remainder of your life?"

Response: "I do."

To Bride: "Please turn to Mark and make this profession of your faith." (Hand card to Victoria. She reads it.)

Bride: "I, Victoria, take you, Mark, to be my husband. I promise before God and these witnesses to be your loving and faithful wife, in plenty and in want, in joy and in sorrow, in adversity and in health, as long as we both shall live."

Presentation of the Rings   Pastor

(Get rings from best man.)

"May I have the rings, please? This ring is a cherished symbol—an outward expression of your faith and a token of your love for one another. This ring is made of gold, a precious metal. It is a perfect, never-ending circle that symbolizes the continuing love of God and the gift of eternal life. These rings serve as a reminder of God's love for you, your love for one another, and the commitment you are making to one another today."

(Give Victoria's ring to Mark.)

To Groom: "Mark, take this ring, place it on Victoria's finger, and as you do, repeat this confession of faith to her:

'With this ring, I thee wed. I give it as a token of my faith and my love, in the name of Jesus.'"

(Give Mark's ring to Victoria.)

To Bride: "Victoria, take this ring, place it on Mark's finger, and as you do, repeat this confession of faith to him:

'With this ring, I thee wed. I give it as a token of my faith and my love, in the name of Jesus.'"

Pronouncement   Pastor

"Join right hands, please. (Pastor puts hand on Mark's and Victoria's hands.) By the authority vested in me as a representative of Jesus Christ and as a minister of His Gospel, and in the name of the Father, of His Son Jesus, and by the power of the Holy Spirit of God, I now pronounce you united together as husband and wife. What God has joined together, let no man put asunder! You may kiss the bride."

(Music begins immediately after the kiss.)

Lighting of the Unity Candle   (While song "Author of Love" plays)

Communion   Pastor

"Mark and Victoria believe that it is important to seal their marriage by sharing communion together. Mark and Victoria serve a living God. Jesus Christ, who has risen from the dead, gives us resurrection power. As you eat this bread and drink this cup, you are again receiving by faith the resurrection power of Jesus Christ to be the husband and wife that God has called you to be."

Song   ("Our Desire")

Prayer and Blessing   Pastor

"Now may the God of patience and comfort grant you to be like-minded toward one another, according to Christ Jesus, that you may with one mind and one mouth glorify the God and Father of our Lord Jesus Christ. Therefore receive one another, just as Christ also received us, to the glory of God" (Romans 15:5-7). (Mark and Victoria turn and face the congregation.)

Presentation of the Bride and Groom   Pastor

"Ladies and gentlemen, I present to you Mr. and Mrs. Mark Windsor!"

Recessional   ("Hallelujah Chorus")

Mark and Victoria exit. Bridal party follows. Ushers come forward.

Pastor signs marriage license and returns vow cards.

Honeymoon Expectations

The honeymoon is a special time. Everyday life is set aside so the two of you are free to enjoy each other. It is important to keep in mind that your focus is not on the things you will be doing, but on the time you will spend together making memories. It should be a time so significant that you will enjoy reminiscing about it for the rest of your lives. This is where expectations come in. Do you expect the honeymoon to be perfect? Will it be without a disagreement or quarrel? Will it be 100 percent romantic? What if either one of you becomes sick?

Here are some questions for you to respond to concerning the honeymoon:
1. Why am I looking forward to our honeymoon?
2. What are my apprehensions concerning our honeymoon?
3. What if the weather does not cooperate?
4. What if our travel plans go awry?
5. What if the menstrual period occurs during our honeymoon?
6. Are we in agreement with what we are doing, where we are going, and how long it will be?
7. Have you scheduled your wedding ceremony early enough in the day so that your wedding night does not begin too late?
8. When will we schedule our second honeymoon?

Probably the sexual relationship comes to mind most often when a couple thinks of their honeymoon. Expectations in this area can either lead to much disappointment or unexpected satisfaction. Please keep in mind that learning to respond to each other sexually is a lifelong process. What you experience on your wedding night and throughout your honeymoon should be unique to you as a couple.

After your honeymoon, be prepared to step back into everyday life with jobs, schedules, and demands being placed upon you. Your honeymoon needs to serve as the foundation for maintaining romance and closeness throughout your Christ-centered marriage. And remember, when you do have disagreements, it will be your opportunity to put into practice what you have learned throughout the premarital program and to experience the beauty of forgiveness and healing.

God's Government in Marriage

The Value of Submission

Before working through this exercise, take a minute to write your personal definition of submission.

_____

_____

_____

_____

God has given man authority over the fish of the sea, the birds, and every living creature (see Gen. 1:28). God placed man in the garden to work and care for His creation (see Gen. 2:15). From the beginning, God has established an order to things. He is not without government. Think of what this world would be like without God's management. God's scriptural basis for order in the Christian marriage is found in Ephesians 5:21-33. Please take time to read these Scriptures. What do we see about God's government in these Scriptures?

1. Men and women are equal in God's eyes, but serve different functions within marriage.
2. The husband is positionally the "head" of the wife. He is responsible to love his wife (see Eph. 5:25); to give up his life for her (see Eph. 5:25); to present his wife to the Lord, holy and cleansed (see Eph. 5:26-27); to love and nurture her as he does himself (see Eph. 5:28); to leave father and mother and become one flesh (see Eph. 5:31).
3. The wife is to submit to her husband (see Eph. 5:22). She is likened to the Body of Christ. The Body of Christ responds in loving submission to Christ (see Eph. 5:22-23). As a wife she is to respond to her husband's love (as Christ loved the church), receive his cleansing, and become one flesh (see Eph. 5:25-26,31). She is to respect her husband (see Eph. 5:33).
4. Submission: What is it? The prefix *sub* means "under." The root word is "mission." Therefore the meaning of submission is to be under the mission.
5. Does the husband force the submission of the wife? No! God spoke these words. It is God who commands, first, "submitting to one another..." (Eph. 5:21) and, second, "wives, submit yourselves to your own husbands, as to the Lord" (Eph. 5:22). Both uses of the word imply

that the one doing the submitting is choosing to place himself or herself under the authority of another.

6. The Greek word for submission in Ephesians 5:21-22 is *hupotasso*. *Hupotasso* is primarily a military term. *Hupo* means "under" and *tasso* means "to arrange." Since Christ has a mission, then men are in submission to Christ's mission. If the husband has a mission, then the wife is in submission to her husband's mission. The man is not more important than the woman, but he is the one responsible before God to be clear about the mission.

7. "Under" does not mean "less than." Imagine a bridge spanning a river valley. Is the bridge merely a road crossing over the water? If it is, it won't stand for long! An extensive support structure *under* the bridge is essential for it to function.

8. Now imagine a train chugging across a prairie. Can the train go anywhere without a track underneath it? Of course not; one cannot function without the other. There can be no attitude of superiority in the husband or the wife.

9. Men, are you clear in your mission? If you are not clear, how can your wife be clear in her role of submission?

10. Let's look at First Peter 3:1-7 to get a better idea of the structure versus the support structure:

    Wives, in the same way be submissive to your husbands so that, if any of them do not believe the word, they may be won over without words by the behavior of their wives, when they see the purity and reverence of your lives. Your beauty should not come from outward adornment, such as braided hair and the wearing of gold jewelry and fine clothes. Instead, it should be that of your inner self, the unfading beauty of a gentle and quiet spirit, which is of great worth in God's sight. For this is the way the holy women of the past who put their hope in God used to make themselves beautiful. They were submissive to their own husbands, like Sarah, who obeyed Abraham and called him her master. You are her daughters if you do what is right and do not give way to fear. Husbands, in the same way be considerate as you live with your wives, and treat them with respect as the weaker partner and as heirs with you of the gracious gift of life, so nothing will hinder your prayers.

11. According to verse 7, men are to honor the woman as the weaker vessel. This does not mean the "less than" vessel. It does not say that the

woman is weaker, but that we are to honor her as the weaker. Physiologically, we know women generally tire more quickly and carry less oxygen in their blood than men. But, if there is a *weaker* vessel, there must be a *weak* vessel as well.

12. God's plan requires the wife to submit and the husband to love. Submitting and loving both require continuous repeated action.

    God has a government. His management of the male/female role is superior to any other system of management. God's order is to cover everyone through His love. "Now I want you to realize that the head of every man is Christ, and the head of the woman is man, and the head of Christ is God....In the Lord, however, woman is not independent of man, nor is man independent of woman. For as woman came from man, so also man is born of woman. But everything comes from God" (1 Cor. 11:3,11-12).

13. Originally God created woman from man. Now man is born of woman. We are not independent of the other. In God's sight, we are equal. Let's face the facts: without woman, none of us would even be here. We are equal, but not the same! "There is neither Jew nor Greek, slave nor free, male nor female, for you are all one in Christ Jesus" (Gal. 3:28). We need one another.

After reading this exercise and studying the Scripture, how has your view of God's government for a husband and wife changed or been challenged?

Endnotes

1. *Merriam-Webster's Collegiate Dictionary*, 11th ed., s.v. "vow."

2. This sample ceremony was adapted from the radio broadcast series, "What Happens at a Wedding," David Mains and Ted Place, October 10-15, 1989. Copyright 1989 by The Chapel of the Air, Inc. Used by permission.

Final Words

We pray that *Called Together* provided you the challenge, wisdom, and fun for building a foundation of marriage that lasts a lifetime. It has been our pleasure to share some of our thoughts, favorite Scriptures, and provocative questions with you. We love marriage and feel that God has given us a wonderful gift worth sharing.

We desire to encourage you as a couple to maintain an open heart toward lifelong enrichment of your marriage. No career is successful without engaging in ongoing training and input. No business prospers without hard work and sacrifices. This is also true of marriage. Read books about marriage, attend marriage seminars and conferences, continue to date, and take weekends away together to simply enjoy one another and have fun together.

It is imperative that you guard your marriage. God has given you to one another and no one else. When you chose your husband or your wife, you said "no" to every other man or woman on the earth. Your commitments to your personal relationship with Jesus and with one another are vital, and you must be on your guard to protect both.

The one constant you can count on in marriage is *change*. Pregnancy may occur, jobs change, children grow up and leave home, an unexpected move occurs. While change is constant, it is rarely something we are totally prepared for. If you find yourselves facing a difficult issue that the two of you cannot resolve, we beg you to seek counsel from your local church or a reputable marriage counselor. While best friends may be helpful, they most likely will not be the most objective. Even the godliest persons need outside input into their lives. It would be immature of us to think we "know it all" or are always right. As we close these pages, we would love to speak some words of blessing over you:

"Our Father, you have blessed us with decades of love, laughter, challenging times, and fruitful times. It has been Your love, Your Word, and our prayer life together that has sustained our marriage through the years and caused our relationship to thrive. While no marriage is perfect, we do serve the Perfect One. Today we speak and impart that same blessing to this precious couple about to embark upon their marriage journey. In Jesus' name, Amen."

Blessings to you,
Steve and Mary Prokopchak

After the Ceremony: Postmarital Section

After the Ceremony

Postmarital training is almost unheard of—but why? The first year of marriage is foundational to a lifelong marriage relationship. There are so many adjustments to make, so many questions that arise. If the premarital instruction was helpful to you, think about how effective the reinforcement of those principles could be, along with accountability to a Christian couple, after you've said, "I do."

God encourages one full year of foundation building. His Word states in Deuteronomy 24:5, "When a man has taken a new wife, he shall not go out to war or be charged with any business; he shall be free at home one year, and bring happiness to his wife whom he has taken" (NKJV). Many couples have confided in us that they took on too much responsibility in their first year of marriage. Taking on more work, ministry, or a side business ended up consuming much of their time and consequently, their year of getting to know one another was quickly stolen from them. Before you enter this first year, assess what you will say "yes" to and what you will say "no" to. Always pray and discuss with one another every opportunity that comes along and guard this foundational year which will help to set the pace for many years to come. Hide Deuteronomy 24:5 in your heart and "bring happiness" to the one whom you have "taken."

This postmarital course can be studied by those newly married or by those who have been married for some time and would like to evaluate their relationship.

Congratulations!

Congratulations are in order again now that you have become one in Jesus Christ. This postmarital course is designed to help you build a firm foundation for your marriage. Please complete the following exercises before Session One (Three Months) and Session Two (Nine Months). Take your assignments seriously, and, again, be honest. If there are areas of conflict within your marriage, there will be no better time than now to pray and work through them.

If personality profiles were used in your premarital counseling, bring them along with your *Called Together* books to postmarital session one. Do not hesitate to ask any question of your postmarital counselors. They are ready and willing to serve you.

> *Have you not read…"For this reason a man shall leave his father and mother and be joined to his wife, and the two shall become one flesh"? So then they are no longer two, but one. Therefore what God has joined together, let not man separate* (Matthew 19:4-6 NKJV).

God bless you, as you've been *Called Together*!

Three Months

Ninety days have come and gone since you spoke that sacred marriage vow to one another. Hopefully it has been the best 90 days of your life. Ninety days seems to be a key term in our society. We hear, for example, the following: "full refund within ninety days if not completely satisfied"; "no interest for ninety days"; "ninety days same as cash." What is being communicated is that in 90 days, reality begins to set in. You have a lifetime to fulfill your commitment to your partner. The honeymoon does not need to come to an end after 90 days. You will begin to learn that romance is a vital element in keeping a marriage relationship fresh and exciting. Don't let your relationship grow stale. Ask the Holy Spirit to remind you of creative ways to express your love: remember special occasions; give flowers, cards, and candy; write love notes, and so forth. Be innovative with your partner. The "reality" is that marriage is a day-to-day commitment.

The first exercise is designed to provoke you into a more knowledgeable communication pattern, while the second exercise provides the opportunity to write about emotional needs. "Scenario Response," the third exercise, will cause you to think about situations in which married couples often find themselves. You will explore ways to be "wise builders" in "Firm Foundation" and give thought to possible personal differences in "Discovering the Differences." One of the final exercises will give you the unique opportunity to share observations about your spouse. "Ways a Husband May Express Love to His Wife" and "Ways a Wife May Express Love to Her Husband" will provide many ideas for demonstrating love to your spouse. You will be given the opportunity to revisit your cooperative marriage mission statement from the premarital counseling sessions. You will also complete an exercise about how the two of you have found yourselves creating a bond with one another.

Expanding Our Communication Knowledge

Read and study this exercise together.

James talks about two kinds of wisdom. He says: "Who is wise and understanding among you? Let him show by good conduct that his works are done in the meekness of wisdom. But if you have bitter envy and self-seeking in your hearts, do not boast and lie against the truth. This wisdom does not descend from above, but is earthly, sensual, demonic" (James 3:13-15 NKJV).

Earthly "wisdom" causes conflict. Envy and selfish ambition give birth to disorder and evil practices. Envying your sister in the Lord because her husband is "more spiritual" than your husband reveals selfish ambition and produces conflict.

"But the wisdom that is from above is first pure, then peaceable, gentle, willing to yield, full of mercy and good fruits, without partiality and without hypocrisy. Now the fruit of righteousness is sown in peace by those who make peace" (James 3:17-18 NKJV).

Heavenly wisdom gives birth to divine order and righteous practices. "Surely He scorns the scornful, but gives grace to the humble" (Prov. 3:34 NKJV). When you respond to your mate with heavenly wisdom (consideration, submission, love, mercy, etc.), envy and selfish ambition must flee: "Therefore submit to God. Resist the devil and he will flee from you" (James 4:7 NKJV). Furthermore, if you sow peace, you will reap a harvest of peace.

James 4:1 raises the question, "What causes fights and quarrels among you?" James's answer is, "Don't they come from your desires that battle within you? You want something but don't get it. You kill and covet, but you cannot have what you want. You quarrel and fight. You do not have, because you do not ask God" (James 4:2).

This passage reveals why we have conflict: we want something, but we are not getting it. Think about any conflict, past or present. You expressed a desire for something. You did not receive it, or you were given something in the place of it. Hurt and/or anger rose within you. You were wronged, taken advantage of, not listened to, or ignored.

Perhaps as a child you wanted a specific kind and color of bicycle for Christmas. What happened when you didn't get what you wanted? Suppose you ask your husband to wash the dishes while you attend a meeting. He forgets, and you have to do them the next morning before work. Suppose you ask your wife to iron your favorite shirt for an important meeting. She gets involved in a lengthy telephone conversation, and you are forced to iron the shirt yourself.

What is important now is your response. Will you become selfish and demanding, even accusing?

You may be tempted to use "you" statements, such as "You're always on the phone." "Can't you ever cook a decent breakfast?" "You're always trying to make me into something I'm not." "You never clean the house." You may also be tempted to use "I told you so" statements: "You continually have to have it your way." "Well, I hope you're satisfied." "Maybe someday you'll learn to take my advice." If you become demanding you will be placing condemnation upon your spouse. Condemnation rarely motivates anyone to do anything. Instead, it causes one to become defensive. Your spouse will interpret your behavior as critical and insensitive and may want to accuse you in return.

These negative "you" statements must be replaced. Avoid using "you" statements when sharing how you feel. Wait until your anger has subsided, then replace "you" statements with "I feel" messages. Let's use two of the "you" statement examples to illustrate this point:

"You" statement	"I feel" message
"You're always on the phone."	"Honey, you probably didn't realize it, but I felt like you didn't care whether or not we would take the time to discuss our Christmas spending limit."
"You're always trying to make me into something I'm not."	"I realize that I'm not perfect and that I have a long way to go, but I really don't understand all the ways that I offend you. I feel like I'm not being accepted for who I am. Can we discuss it?" When demanding our way, we often use words that tear down rather than edify. Resist that selfish desire, and submit your communication to God. As husband and wife, you need to hold one another accountable for how you make each other feel. You must have the courage to reveal how you feel through a soft "answer" in order to avoid criticizing and creating defensive attitudes.

"Anyone, then, who knows the good he ought to do and doesn't do it, sins" (James 4:17). List some of the "you" statements that you may have spoken to your spouse, and turn them into "I feel" messages.

"You" statement	"I feel" message
_____	_____
_____	_____
_____	_____
_____	_____
_____	_____
_____	_____

Complete the following questions individually.

1. How do you tend to handle conflict in your life?_____
    _____

2. Where did you learn this pattern of dealing with conflict?_____
    _____

3. Recall the most recent conflict that you experienced with your spouse. What was it?_____
    _____

4. What was your desired outcome from this conflict?_____
    _____

5. What did your spouse desire in the conflict?_____
    _____

6. How did you bring this conflict to a resolution?_____
    _____
    _____

Emotional Needs

Complete the following without the input of your spouse.

    A.   List ten of your personal emotional needs. (Examples of emotional needs might include appreciation, affection, respect, and honesty.)

        1.

        2.

        3.

        4.

        5.

        6.

        7.

        8.

        9.

        10.

    B.   List ten of your spouse's personal emotional needs.

        1.

        2.

        3.

        4.

        5.

        6.

        7.

        8.

        9.

        10.

    C.   Do you feel as though your spouse misinterprets your emotional needs? If yes, explain:

The goal is not to feel as though we must meet every emotional need that our spouse expresses or has. We must first learn to look to God to have our emotional needs met; however, identifying those needs in our lives will help us to understand ourselves and our spouses better. This understanding can enable us to help meet our spouse's emotional needs.

Scenario Response

Complete this exercise individually.

1. How is the "ideal" marriage different from your marriage?
2. Because of a greater familiarity with your spouse, you now feel tempted to say things or do things you would not have considered saying or doing during your engagement. How will you handle this temptation? Imagine the following scenarios:
3. You have taken the time to communicate some important information to your spouse. Your spouse did not hear you the first time, so you are now repeating your statement. In the middle of repeating this information a second time, your spouse says rather bluntly, "Would you stop mumbling and speak up so I can hear you?" What is your response?
4. You and your spouse have agreed to spend $75 per week on groceries. Your partner returns home from grocery shopping ecstatic about "all the great deals." You ask, "How much did you spend?" His/her reply is "$95." What is your response?
5. You have communicated a desire for sexual relations. Your spouse also seems to agree excitedly. In the middle of your evening prayer time, your spouse falls asleep. This would be OK except that this is the third night in a row that this has happened. What is your response?

Firm Foundation

Please complete this exercise with your spouse.

Read Matthew 7:24-27. Jesus describes the wise and the foolish builders. Take the time to describe the areas in which the two of you see yourselves building upon a firm foundation for marriage.

1.
2.
3.

As discussed in the premarital counseling sessions, a vital part of this firm foundation is couple prayer. Please take the time to address your prayer life together as a couple. What are your prayer goals for the future?

Discovering the Differences

Complete this exercise without the help of your spouse.

1. Have you discovered any likes or dislikes on the part of your spouse that you were not aware of before marriage? Please elaborate.

   Remember that Paul wrote in Second Corinthians 5:17 that we are becoming a new creation.

2. Are your mate's moral and spiritual values what you thought they were before you were married?

   Jesus said in Matthew 6:21 that where our treasure is our heart will be also.

3. Have you discovered any behavioral changes, positive or negative, in yourself or your spouse since marriage?

   Romans 15:7 says to accept one another. James 1:22-24 admonishes us to be doers of the Word.

4. Have you discovered any habits (good or not so good) in yourself or in your mate that you were not aware of before marriage? Please elaborate.

   First Thessalonians 5:15 admonishes us to make sure that nobody pays back wrong for wrong, but to be kind to each other.

5. Have you discovered any problems from your past that are now manifesting in your marriage?

   Galatians 5:1 tells us that Christ set us free for freedom's sake. God also states in Micah 7:18-19 that He delights in mercy and compassion. Ephesians 4:17-25 encourages us to put off the old and put on the new.

Perceptions of My Spouse

Below you are given the opportunity to evaluate your spouse. Be honest in your evaluation and remember that these are just your perceptions...

	Needs to Improve	Improving	Good	Very Good
1. Decision-making				
2. Conflict resolution				
3. Finances				
4. Jealousy				
5. Hobbies (time balanced)				
6. Moodiness				
7. Temper				
8. Dependability				
9. Job (responsibility)				
10. Recreation (time balanced)				
11. Television (time balanced)				
12. Telephone				
13. Affection				
14. Friendships				
15. Praying together				
16. Spending time with you				
17. Relatives (relationships)				
18. Sense of humor				
19. Time with God				
20. Communication				

Postmarital Marriage Mission Statement

In Session One of your premarital counseling, you wrote an individual mission statement. In Session Two, you created a cooperative mission statement. Please copy that cooperative mission statement below.

_____

_____

_____

_____

_____

_____

_____

_____

_____

_____

Does this mission statement that you have written apply to your marriage today, or are there changes that need to be considered? Together make revisions; then rewrite a new mission statement.

_____

_____

_____

_____

_____

_____

_____

_____

_____

_____

Using your mission statement as a focal point, record your top three to five priorities. These priorities may include relationships, activities, finances, spiritual service, or personal concerns found within your mission statement.

1.
2.
3.
4.
5.

How can you pray together as a couple to see this mission accomplished?

_____

_____

_____

_____

_____

Are there some goals that you can develop in writing that will move you toward your cooperative mission statement?

Goal #1

Goal #2

Goal #3

We have a tendency to become preoccupied with the things we do in this world, and we can easily be distracted from our life mission. Review your cooperative mission statement from time to time so you can maintain a clear focus and direction in your call together.

Be aware that the longer you are married, the greater the chance that your marriage mission statement will change significantly. As it changes, you will be able to rejoice over needs met and answers to prayer. With each season of marriage comes new freedoms and new challenges. Remember, when we press through adversities together, our marriage relationship grows closer to God and to one another.

Bonding and Boundaries

God created us to have and enjoy relationship. Close relationships go through a process of bonding. When a bond is broken by crossing boundaries that we are not to cross, we can move toward bondage. When Adam and Eve disobeyed God's boundaries, they moved from a very close bond with one another and with

God to a fallen state of bondage. Throughout your married lives there will be a delicate balance that needs to be maintained between bonding and boundaries. Both are necessary for a growing, maturing marriage. Together consider the questions below and write your response in the space provided.

1. In what ways as a couple have we bonded together? (example: looking to God together rather than looking to our parents)

2. What are some of the boundaries that we have discovered will be important to maintain? (example: making a phone call to our spouse concerning a change in our schedule)

3. When you said "yes" to each other on your wedding day, you also said "no" to all other sexual or deeply close emotional relationships. Write about how you will maintain your marital (sexual) and emotional boundaries.

Praying for Your Spouse

Mary and I have discovered a key ingredient to a richly blessed marriage relationship—prayer. Praying for one another, praying for our children, and praying with one another has provided a spiritual intimacy like no other. Our relationship has been challenged, stretched, deepened, and encouraged by seeking our heavenly Father together. Prayer is a place of power and agreement. Prayer builds intimacy as we hear one another's heart. Prayer is a unifying force. We worry less because we pray. We communicate at a deeper level because we pray. We grow more in love because we pray. We experience committed union "until death do us part" because we pray. May we challenge you to discover this place of security as you discover a new release in praying God's Word.

With a spirit of faith I pray . . . . 2 Corinthians 4:13

Peace of Mind

Surely goodness and love will follow my spouse
all the days of his/her life . . . . Psalm 23:6
My spouse has great peace and nothing can make
him/her stumble . . . . Psalm 119:165
My spouse's work will be rewarded . . . . Jeremiah 31:16
Keep my spouse's mind in perfect peace because
his/her trust is in you . . . . Isaiah 26:3
Nothing will separate us from the love of God
that is in Christ Jesus our Lord . . . . Romans 8:38-39
My spouse will not become weary in doing
good and will reap a harvest . . . . Galatians 6:9
May the peace of Christ rule in my spouse's heart. . . Colossians 3:15
My spouse will submit himself/herself to God
and resist the devil . . . . James 4:7
As my spouse and I love one another, God lives in
us, and His love is made complete in us . . . . 1 John 4:12
My spouse will overcome the devil by the blood of
the Lamb and by the word of his/her testimony. Revelation 12:11
The Lord bless, keep and be gracious to my spouse . Numbers 6:24-26

Protection and Freedom From Fear

My spouse who seeks the Lord lacks no good thing . . . . Psalm 34:10
No harm will befall you; no disaster will come near you. Psalm 91:10
Do not fear or be dismayed; God will strengthen
you and help you. . . . . Isaiah 41:10

No weapon formed against my spouse will prevail . . . . . Isaiah 54:17

My spouse has the mind of Christ . . . . 1 Corinthians 2:16

Satan will not outwit my spouse, for we are not
    unaware of his schemes. . . . . 2 Corinthians 2:11

By Your faithfulness You will strengthen and
    protect my spouse from the evil one . . . . 2 Thessalonians 3:3

For God did not give my spouse a spirit of timidity,
    but a spirit of power, love, and self-discipline . . . . . 2 Timothy 1:7

The Lord is my spouse's helper; what can man do? . . . Hebrews 13:6

My spouse will not walk in fear, for perfect love
    drives out fear . . . . 1 John 4:18

My spouse's enemies will turn back when I call for help . Psalm 56:9

God is God, and He is faithful to my spouse, keeping
    His covenant to a thousand generations . . . . Deuteronomy 7:9

Restoration and Healing

My spouse will not die, but live and proclaim
    what the Lord has done . . . . Psalm 118:17

Weeping may remain for a night, but rejoicing comes
    in the morning to my spouse . . . . Psalm 30:5

He heals the brokenhearted and binds up my
    spouse's wounds . . . . Psalm 147:3

Our love covers all wrongs. . . . . Proverbs 10:12

May my spouse live by every word that comes
    from the mouth of God. . . . . Matthew 4:4

Give my spouse a new attitude, created to be like
    God in true righteousness and holiness . . . . . . Ephesians 4:23-24

Never will You leave, never will You forsake
    my spouse. . . . . Hebrews 13:5

May my spouse enjoy good health, and may
    all go well with him/her . . . . 3 John 2

May my spouse trust in and delight her/himself
    in the Lord . . . . Psalm 37:3-4

Grace and Faith

My wife will be a fruitful vine within my house . . . . . . Psalm 128:3

As for me and my household, we will serve the Lord. . . Joshua 24:15

My spouse will love the Lord God, walk in all
    His ways, obey His commands, hold fast to Him,
    and serve Him with all his/her heart and soul . . . . . . Joshua 22:5

There is no condemnation over my spouse . . . . Romans 8:1

Increase my spouse's store of seed, and enlarge the
harvest of his/her righteousness . . . . 2 Corinthians 9:10

My spouse lives by faith and not by sight . . . . 2 Corinthians 5:7

God's grace is sufficient for my spouse, and His
power is made perfect in weakness . . . . 2 Corinthians 12:9

God has begun a good work in my spouse and
will complete it . . . . Philippians 1:6

We will be like-minded, having the same love,
being one in the spirit and purpose, in humility
considering my spouse as better than myself . . . Philippians 2:2-3

My spouse can do everything through Him who
gives my spouse strength . . . . Philippians 4:13

Nine Months

Your first anniversary is just three months away! You have been married for almost a year! How are you feeling about your marriage, your spouse, and the foundation you have been building for the past nine months? Are you meeting the goals you established for your first year of marriage? Are you feeling disillusioned in any areas of your marriage relationship?

This nine-month checkup will assist you as a couple to reevaluate your goals, priorities, finances, communication patterns, and sexual relationship. Challenge yourselves to pursue a new level of commitment in your marriage relationship as you proceed through the following exercises.

The first exercise, "Differences and Similarities in Relationship," focuses on your strengths and weaknesses as a couple, while the second exercise provides a candid approach to discussing various areas of marriage. The next exercise centers on sexual relations, while the "Goals" exercise provides an opportunity to consider your goals together. You are also given space to rework your annual budget. The postmarital study concludes with a discussion of the three parts of human beings and with one of the most important topics of marriage—forgiveness. Enjoy yourselves.

Differences and Similarities in Relationship

Complete this exercise as a couple.

1. Discuss the ways in which you are opposites. How can these differences strengthen your relationship? Discuss how the enemy (satan) would like to use these differences to weaken your relationship.
2. What gifts does your spouse have that you do not have?
3. Discuss several incidents that have drawn you closer to your spouse.
4. How can you tell when your spouse is unhappy with you?
5. Which one of you is more task-oriented? Which one of you is more relational? Discuss how this can be a strength, as well as a weakness.

6. Discuss the ways in which you as a couple are similar. How do these similarities strengthen your relationship?

For Further Discussion

Complete the following without the help of your spouse.

1. In what ways are you still tied to your parents?
2. Do you as a couple have other couples as close friends?
3. Do you as an individual still maintain close, same-sex friendships? Do you have a "best" friend?
4. Do you enjoy your job? Does your spouse support you working where you do? Do you have a tendency to bring work frustrations home with you?
5. In what ways do you feel your spouse is dependent upon you?
6. Is there something that you do not understand about your spouse?
7. In what ways are you secure in your spouse's commitment?
8. a. How have you attempted to change your spouse?
   b. How has your spouse attempted to change you?
9. Does your spouse consider your feelings before making a decision?
10. Are there any ways in which you feel as though you have failed to meet your spouse's needs?
11. Please list your first five priorities (for example: job, spouse, God, mother, children, ministry).
12. Are there any activities in your spouse's life that you feel are more important than you are?
13. Are there any ways in which you feel as though your spouse has failed to meet your needs?
14. Have you hurt or offended your spouse in any way?
15. Is your spouse willing to admit that he/she is wrong?
16. Is your spouse willing to apologize?
17. Can your spouse accept advice/counsel from you? From others?
18. Does your spouse have any negative habits or attitudes that have affected your marriage?
19. Is your spouse still emotionally tied to his/her parents in an unhealthy way?
20. a. How much time do you as an individual and as a couple spend watching television?
    b. What effect does television have on your marriage relationship? _____ strong effect _____ average effect _____ little effect

21. Are you and your spouse taking time for regular date nights?
22. Have you and your spouse scheduled any overnight getaways since you have been married?

Sexual Communication Exercise

Complete the following without the input of your spouse. Please be honest in your answers. Answer by marking a check in the yes (most of the time), no (seldom), or sometimes column.

	Yes	No	Some-times
1. Do you enjoy your sexual relationship?			
2. Do you feel that your partner enjoys your sexual relationship?			
3. Do you and your partner agree on the frequency of sexual intercourse?			
4. Do you understand your partner's sexual needs and desires?			
5. Does your partner understand your sexual needs and desires?			
6. Do you make your sexual needs known to your partner?			
7. Does your partner make his/her sexual needs known to you?			
8. Do you and your partner take sufficient time to engage in foreplay?			
9. Do you avoid discussing any sexual areas or needs?			
10. Do you feel your partner avoids discussing any sexual areas?			
11. Have you discussed sexual problems with anyone other than your spouse?			
12. Is it difficult for you to ask your partner to engage in sex?			
13. Do you and your partner pray about your sexual relationship?			
14. Have you and your partner studied any books on the sexual union?			
15. Is your partner affectionate with you outside of sexual intercourse?			
16. Are you affectionate with your partner outside of sexual intercourse?			

	Yes	No	Some-times
17. Do you and your partner discuss problems within your sexual relationship?	_____	_____	_____
18. Have you ever refused to fulfill your partner's sexual request?	_____	_____	_____
19. Has your partner ever refused to fulfill a sexual request from you?	_____	_____	_____
20. Are you able to share with your partner what you find enjoyable sexually?	_____	_____	_____
21. Does your partner share with you what he/she finds enjoyable sexually?	_____	_____	_____

Complete these statements.

22. Our sex life has been _____

23. Sexually I wish _____

24. In the future I hope our sex life will _____

25. Some suggestions that I have for building intimacy in our relationship are

_____

_____

_____

Goals

You may feel that it is too soon to begin looking at life goals. But as the saying goes, "If you aim for nothing, you'll always hit it." Goals are important. In *Training Christians to Counsel*, Norm Wright states that a good goal "must have three characteristics: (1) it must be specific (well-defined, to the point); (2) it must be realistic, or attainable; (3) it must have a time limit (next week, this summer, in twenty years—someday does not count)."[1]

Example Goal:

We desire to pay our home off completely within ten years (well-defined and attainable with a specific time frame). We will pay an extra $200 per month for ten years and place each year's tax return on the principal payment (the "how" is now defined). We will ask Rob's father to hold us accountable in accomplishing this goal (an appropriate accountability measure).

List, as a couple, several goals in the areas indicated. Please remember to be specific and realistic and to set a time limit.

  A. Spiritual goals (example: a mission team trip, individual devotional time)
  B. Physical goals (example: to exercise, to be more sexually responsive)
  C. Financial goals (example: to save $100 per paycheck, to purchase a house)
  D. Family goals (example: when to start our family, number of children)
  E. Employment goals (example: to be branch manager)

Perceptions of My Spouse

Below you are given the opportunity to evaluate your spouse. Be honest and remember that these are just your perceptions. Compare them with your three-month responses. Is there improvement?

	Needs to Improve	Improving	Good	Very Good
1. Decision-making				
2. Conflict resolution				
3. Finances				
4. Jealousy				
5. Hobbies (time balanced)				
6. Moodiness				
7. Temper				
8. Dependability				
9. Job (responsibility)				
10. Recreation (time balanced)				
11. Television (time balanced)				
12. Telephone				
13. Affection				
14. Friendships				
15. Praying together				
16. Spending time with you				
17. Relatives (relationships)				
18. Sense of humor				
19. Time with God				
20. Communication				

Personal Finances Budget

Since two incomes merge into one after marriage, it is important to once again revisit the financial budget sheet. As a couple, you should now have a more complete picture of your financial needs and goals.

You will need to locate an appropriate time and place to begin reworking your proposed budget. It is a good idea to pray before you begin. Commit your finances to God, and determine to work together in financial agreement. It may take several hours of your time to complete. Seeing the overall and updated picture can be extremely helpful. After completion you may want to review the figures and make necessary adjustments. While a budget sheet will never stop you from spending your money, it will give you an honest picture of where your cash is going and exactly what your income is.

Make several copies of the next page, or use it as an example to create a spreadsheet on your computer. For line item details and a completed sample, refer back to the premarital "Personal Finances Budget."

Personal Finances Budget Sheet

Category	Jan	Feb	Mar	April	May	June	July	August	Sept	Oct	Nov	Dec	Amount Total	Average Total
Income: Husband														
Wife														
Tithe														
Federal Tax														
State Tax														
County Tax														
Investment / FICA														
Mortgage														
Rent														
Maintenance														
Electricity														
Heat														
Water														
Sewer														
Trash														
Telephone / Internet														
Food & Supplies														
Clothing														
Auto Payment / Lease														
Auto Gas														
Auto Insurance														
Auto License / Reg.														
Auto Maintenance														
Medical / Dental														
Gifts														
Dining														
Travel / Vacation														
Rec / Entertainment														
Education														
Subscriptions														
Health / Life Insurance														
Debt														
Miscellaneous														
Giving														
Savings														
Cumulative Savings														

Three Parts of Humankind

Read and study together.

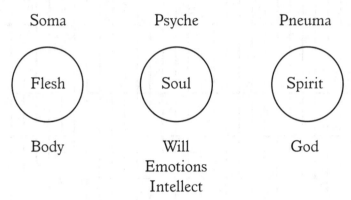

Soma	Psyche	Pneuma
Flesh	Soul	Spirit
Body	Will	God
	Emotions	
	Intellect	

We know God as Father, Son, and Holy Spirit. Just as God is three in one, so are we whom He created. God has designed humankind with flesh, our body which will return to the dust of the earth (see Gen. 3:19); soul, our will, emotions, and intellect (see Ezek. 18:4; Matt. 10:28); and spirit (see Gen. 1:27; 1 Thess. 5:23).

This illustration clarifies God's design for marriage. If the marriage is built in the fleshly realm (the lust of the eyes, the lust of the flesh—see First John 2:16), it will not endure. Before long this marriage will experience tremendous difficulty. There is much more to a relationship than the physical act of sex.

When a marriage is built in the soul realm, it may also be short-lived. Two college graduates may be able to communicate on a very intelligent level, but this alone will not be enough to sustain the relationship. If a decision to marry was made out of a strong will or during an "emotional high," this too will soon fade.

However, when a marriage is built in the spiritual realm, it is off to a powerful start. The Bible clearly indicates that God the Father, God the Son, and God the Spirit agree as one (see 1 John 5:8). Amos 3:3 states, "Can two walk together, unless they are agreed?" This agreement must first take place in the spiritual realm. Now let's look together at Matthew 18:19: "Again, I [Jesus] say to you that if two of you on earth agree concerning anything that they ask, it will be done for them by My Father in heaven" (NKJV). The Bible indicates that when the two of you agree, it will be done. This is why a marriage built in the spiritual realm is so powerful.

If the two of you agree in prayer about a financial need, a physical need, an emotional need, or a spiritual need according to God's will, it will be done. There is power in your agreement. Consequently, the key is not to argue about the need but to pray and agree.

When a marriage is built in the spirit, all of hell cannot touch it. The enemy loves to attack our flesh and our soul, but when we are built up in the spirit, we need not give him any ground.

Discuss areas in which you have discovered the power of agreement with your spouse.

Prayerfully list some areas in which you feel agreement still needs to be actively pursued.

Can you as a couple disagree and still be in unity?

Ways a Husband May Express Love to His Wife[2]

How to Convince Your Wife You Love Her

1. Function as the loving leader of your home.
2. Frequently tell her you love her.
3. If she does not work outside the home, give her an agreed-upon amount of money to spend in any way she chooses.
4. Lead family devotions regularly.
5. Do something spontaneous and zany—don't always be predictable.
6. Share the household chores.
7. Take care of the children for at least three hours every week so that she has free time to do whatever she wants.
8. Take her out for dinner or to do some fun thing at least once a week.
9. Do the "fix-it" jobs she wants done around the house.
10. Greet her when you come home with a smile, a hug, a kiss, and an "Am I glad to see you. I really missed you today."
11. Give her a lingering kiss.
12. Pat her on the shoulder, hold her hand, and caress her frequently.
13. Be willing to talk to her about her concerns, and don't belittle her for having them.
14. Look at her with an adoring expression.
15. Sit close to her.
16. Rub her back.
17. Shave, take a shower, and brush your teeth before you have sexual relations.
18. Wear her favorite after-shave lotion.
19. Write love notes or letters to her.
20. Let her know you appreciate her and what you appreciate about her. Do this often and for things that are sometimes taken for granted.
21. Fulfill her implied or unspoken wishes as well as the specific requests she makes of you.
22. Anticipate what she might like, and surprise her by doing it before she asks.
23. Play together; share her hobbies and recreational preferences enthusiastically; include her in yours.
24. Set a good example before the children.
25. Talk about her favorably to the children when she can hear you, and even when she cannot.
26. Brag about her good points to others; let her know you are proud to have her as your wife.
27. Maintain your own spiritual life through Bible study, prayer, regular church attendance, and fellowship with God's people.

28. Structure your time and use it wisely; be on time to go places.
29. Make plans prayerfully and carefully.
30. Ask her advice when you have problems or decisions to make.
31. Follow her advice unless to do so would violate biblical principles.
32. Fulfill your responsibilities.
33. Be sober, but not somber, about life.
34. Have a realistic, biblical, positive attitude toward life.
35. Discuss plans with your wife before you make decisions, and when the plans are made, share them fully with your wife, giving reasons for making the decisions you did.
36. Thank her in creative ways for her attempts to please you.
37. Ask forgiveness often, and say, "I was wrong and will try to change."
38. Actually change areas of your life that you know need changing.
39. Share your insights and good experiences with her.
40. Plan a mini-honeymoon.
41. Give some expression of admiration when she wears a new dress or your favorite negligee.
42. Gently brush her leg under the table.
43. Be reasonably happy to go shopping with her.
44. Relate what happened at work or whatever you did apart from her.
45. Reminisce about the early days of your marriage.
46. Express appreciation for her parents and relatives.
47. Take her out to breakfast.
48. Agree with her about getting a new dress or some other item.
49. Thank her when she supports your decisions and cooperates enthusiastically. Especially make it a matter of celebration when she supports and helps enthusiastically at times when you know she doesn't fully agree.
50. Ask her to have sexual relations with you, and seek to be especially solicitous of her desires. Express gratitude when she tries to please you.
51. Buy gifts for her.
52. Remember anniversaries and other events that are special to her.
53. Watch the television program she wants to watch, or go where she wants to go instead of doing what you want to do. Do it cheerfully and enthusiastically.
54. Be cooperative and appreciative when she holds you, caresses, or kisses you.
55. Be cooperative when she tries to arouse you and desires to have sexual relations. Never make fun of her for expressing her desires.
56. Run errands gladly.
57. Pamper her, and make a fuss over her.

58. Be willing to see things from her point of view.
59. Be lovingly honest with her—no withholding of the truth that may hinder your present or future relationship.
60. Indicate you want to be alone with her and talk or just lie in each other's arms.
61. Refuse to "cop out," "blow up," attack, shift blame, withdraw, or exaggerate when she seeks to make constructive suggestions or discuss problems.
62. Give her your undivided attention when she wants to talk.
63. Cheerfully stay up past your bedtime to solve problems or share her burdens.
64. Get up in the middle of the night to take care of the children so that she may continue to sleep.
65. Hold her close while expressing tangible and vocal love when she is hurt, discouraged, weary, or burdened.
66. Plan vacations and trips with her.
67. Help her yourself instead of telling the children to "help Mommy."
68. Be eager to share a good joke or some other interesting information you have learned.
69. Join with her in a team ministry in the church.
70. Do a Bible study or research project together.
71. Establish a family budget.
72. Keep yourself attractive and clean.
73. Be a cooperative, helpful host when you have people over for dinner or fellowship.
74. Ask her to pray with you about something.
75. Spend time with the children in play, study, and communication.
76. Acknowledge that there are some specific areas or ways in which you need to improve.
77. Refuse to disagree with her in the presence of others.
78. Cooperate with her in establishing family goals and then in fulfilling them.
79. Be available and eager to fulfill her desires whenever and wherever possible and proper.
80. Begin each day with cheerfulness and tangible expressions of affection.
81. Plan to spend some time alone with her for sharing and communicating every day.
82. Remember to tell her when you must work late.
83. Refuse to work late on a regular basis.
84. Take care of the yard work properly.
85. Help the children with their homework.
86. Refuse to compare her unfavorably with other people.
87. Handle money wisely.
88. Don't allow work, church, or recreational activities to keep you from

fulfilling marriage or family responsibilities.

89. Try to find things to do with her.
90. Be willing to go out or stay home with her.
91. Be polite to her.
92. Refuse to be overly dependent on your parents or friends.
93. Develop mutual friends.
94. Provide adequate health and life insurance.
95. Keep her vehicle properly maintained.
96. Be especially helpful when she is not feeling well.
97. Be on time.
98. Go to parent/teacher conferences with her.
99. Let her sleep in once in a while by feeding the children breakfast and, if possible, getting them off to school.
100. Frequently give in to her and allow her to have her own way, unless to do so would be sinful.
101. Put the children to bed at night.
102. Be gentle and tender, and hold her before and after sexual relations.
103. Don't nit-pick and find fault, and don't give the impression that you expect her to be perfect.
104. Surprise her with an overnight stay in a local motel.
105. Send her an e-mail, or call her cell phone telling her how much you love and miss her today.

Evaluate the way you express your love to your wife. Go over this list and circle any ways you may be neglecting to show love for your wife. Ask your wife to go over the list and put a check mark in front of the ways she would like you to express love. Ask her to add other things to the list.

As a newly married wife, are there any other ways not expressed in this list that you desire your husband to express love to you?

_____

_____

_____

_____

_____

_____

_____

_____

_____

_____

Ways a Wife
May Express Love to Her Husband[2]

How to Convince Your Husband You Love Him

1. Greet him at the door when he comes home with a smile, a hug, a kiss, and an "Am I glad to see you. I really missed you today."

2. Have a cup of coffee or tea ready for him when he comes home from work or a trip.

3. Give him a lingering kiss.

4. Let him know you like to be with him, and make arrangements so that you can spend time with him without giving the impression that you really should or would rather be doing something else.

5. Be willing to talk to him about his concerns without belittling him for having these concerns.

6. Support him and cooperate with him enthusiastically when he has made a decision.

7. Tease and flirt with him.

8. Seek to arouse him and sometimes be the aggressor in sexual relations.

9. Ask him to have sexual relations more than he would expect you to.

10. Express yourself passionately during sexual relations.

11. Caress him.

12. Look at him with an adoring expression.

13. Sit close to him.

14. Hold his hand.

15. Rub his back.

16. Wear his favorite nightgown or dress or perfume.

17. Express your love in words or notes.

18. Let him know you appreciate him and what you appreciate about him. Do this often and for things that are sometimes taken for granted.

19. Frequently fulfill his unspoken wishes as well as the specific requests he makes of you. Try to anticipate what he might like and surprise him by doing it before he asks.

20. Play together (tennis, golf, party games, etc.).

21. Enthusiastically share with him in devotions and prayer; seek to set a good example for the children concerning their attitude toward devotions and prayer.

22. Maintain your own spiritual life through Bible study and prayer.

23. Structure your time and use it wisely.

24. Be willing to face and solve problems even if it requires discomfort, change, and much effort.

25. Fulfill your responsibilities.

26. Ask him for his advice and frequently follow it.

27. Be ready to leave at the appointed time.

28. Stand with him and support him in his attempts to raise your children for God.

29. Thank him in creative ways for his attempts to please you.

30. Ask for forgiveness; say, "I was wrong and will try to change."

31. Actually change areas of your life that you know need changing.

32. Work with him on his projects.

33. Read books or magazine articles he asks you to read, and share your insights.

34. Let him know when he has to make decisions that you really believe he will choose the right thing and that you will wholeheartedly support him in whatever decision he makes, provided the decision does not violate clearly revealed biblical principles. Be his best cheerleader and fan.

35. Buy gifts for him.

36. Show genuine interest in his hobbies; watch or attend sporting events with him; listen to him sing and play the guitar or piano; attend a class he teaches.

37. Find a mutually agreeable way to keep the house neat and clean.

38. Cook creative and nutritious meals—or praise him when he does.

39. Have devotions with the children when he is not able to be there.

40. Maintain his disciplinary rules when he is not present.

41. Be cooperative and appreciative when he holds you, caresses, or kisses you.

42. Lovingly give him your input when you think he is in error.

43. Offer constructive suggestions when you think he could improve or become more productive. Don't push or preach or do this in such a way that you belittle him, but seek positive and nonthreatening ways to help him become more fully the man God wants him to be.

44. Run errands gladly.

45. Seek to complete him, not compete with him; be the best member on his team, and seek to convince him that you are just that.

46. Be lovingly honest with him—no withholding of the truth that may hinder your relationship or future trust and closeness.

47. Be willing to see things from his point of view; believe the best about what he does or says.

48. Pamper him, and make a fuss over him.

49. Be happy and cheerful.

50. Refuse to nag.

51. Gently brush his leg under the table.

52. Have candlelight and music at dinner.

53. Indicate you want to be alone with him to talk or just lie in his arms.

54. Give a "suggestive" wink.

55. Go for a walk with him.

56. Let him know you feel lonely when he is out of town.

57. Tell him about your work day.

58. Share your fears, concerns, joys, failures, and so forth.

59. Seek to support your ideas with biblical insights and practical wisdom.

60. Refuse to "cop out," withdraw, attack, exaggerate, or shift blame when he seeks to make constructive suggestions or discuss problems.

61. Give him your undivided attention when he wants to talk.

62. Discuss the meaning of certain Bible passages, or discuss how to improve your marriage, home, children, or child-raising efforts.

63. Cheerfully stay up past your bedtime to resolve a disagreement or problem.

64. Hold him close while expressing tangible and vocal love when he is hurt, discouraged, weary, or burdened.

65. Be eager to share a good joke or some other interesting information you have learned.

66. Work in the yard, paint a room together, or wash the car.

67. Plan vacations or trips together.

68. Keep your family memorabilia, newspaper clippings, church bulletins.

69. Brag to others about his accomplishments, and tell them what a good husband he is.

70. Join with him in a team ministry in the church.

71. Do a Bible study or research project together.

72. Keep up with family finances.

73. Help prepare the income tax report.

74. Keep in touch with your family and friends through letters.

75. Keep yourself attractive and clean.

76. Invite his friends or work associates over for dinner or fellowship.

77. Develop and use the spiritual gifts God has given you.

78. Ask him to pray with you.

79. Express how much you love the children, and be their cheerleader.

80. Stay within the family budget; save some money for special surprises.

81. Be excited about sharing the Gospel, celebrating answered prayer, or helping other people.

82. Make a list of things that need to be done around the house.

83. Be satisfied with your present standard of living, furniture, and appliances when you cannot afford to upgrade them.

84. Don't make nostalgic comments about your father that might imply that you think your father is a much better man than your husband.

85. Acknowledge that there are some specific areas in which you need to improve.

86. Appreciate and help his family.

87. Refuse to disagree with him in the presence of others.
88. Cooperate with him in establishing family goals.
89. Be unconventional in your love-making.
90. Tell him before he asks that you think he has done a good job. Don't be afraid of repeating yourself in commending him for what he is or does.
91. Be available and eager to fulfill his desires whenever and wherever possible and proper.
92. Begin each day with cheerfulness and tangible expressions of affection.
93. Let the children know that you and your husband agree; communicate to your children when you husband can hear (and when he cannot) how wonderful he is.
94. Do something spontaneous and zany—don't always be predictable.
95. Send cards to him at his workplace.
96. Stuff his suitcase with love notes when he travels.
97. Surprise him by cooking his favorite dinner.
98. Call him and tell him if you're going to be late from work or a meeting.
99. Read a couple's devotional together before bedtime.
100. Place a love note on his car at his work place.
101. Call him on his cell phone just to tell him you love and miss him.
102. Surprise him with an unexpected overnight at a local motel.
103. Go for a walk together hand in hand.
104. Send him an e-mail, and communicate what a wonderful husband he is.
105. Plan with the children a "daddy appreciation" night.

Evaluate the way you express your love to your husband. Go over this list, and circle any ways you may be neglecting to show love for your husband. Ask your husband to go over the list and put a check mark in front of the ways he would like you to express love. Ask him to add other things to the list.

As a newly married husband, are there any other ways not expressed in this list that you desire your wife to express love to you?

_____

_____

_____

_____

_____

Forgiveness: A Final Word

Jesus taught us in Matthew 6:14-15 that if we forgive others, the Lord will forgive us. You choose whether or not to forgive. As someone appropriately said, forgiveness is God's medicine. You will feel at times that the person who has angered you does not deserve forgiveness. Jesus did not say to forgive only those who deserve forgiveness. Forgiveness releases you, as well as the one who wronged you.

Forgiveness is an important ingredient in a marriage. Anyone in close relationship with another will encounter times of stress and frustration. It is at these times that we may say the wrong thing or behave in the wrong way. The following is a practical, step-by-step, scripturally based process for forgiveness.

This exercise completes the formal postmarital training. However, it is our hope that you will continue accountability, prayer, Bible study, and an ongoing desire to grow in your relationship with Christ and with each other. God bless you in your call together.

Seven Steps to Forgiveness

Anger can be a legitimate response. After the reaction of anger has been dealt with, we can then move toward forgiveness.

1. **Choose to Forgive.**

    Forgiveness begins with a simple decision that, in Jesus' name, we will obey God and forgive those who have hurt us:

    And be kind to one another, tenderhearted, forgiving one another, even as God in Christ forgave you (Ephesians 4:32).

    Jesus made it clear in Matthew 18:35 that this decision to forgive is to be from the heart. We are to forgive wholeheartedly, not holding back or keeping any resentment.

    But what about feelings? Here are some helps in dealing with them.

    - Forgiveness starts not with feelings, but with a decision. You don't need to wait for the right feeling before deciding to forgive. Instead, you can forgive! You can choose to forgive from your heart, and God will recognize that. Verbalize this decision: by faith confess aloud, "In Jesus' name I forgive _____." When you have done this, your feelings will be moving toward a resolve.

    - Be alert! Satan may try to bring some feelings of resentment back into your life (see 1 Pet. 5:8-10). You do not need to feel guilty about these temptations, but you do need to deal with them. Since you have already made your choice, you need to stand firm on having already forgiven that person in Jesus' name.

- When that feeling of resentment comes back, say to yourself, "I did forgive! I dealt with that." Eventually when you remember that sad experience, it will be with the happy thought, "That's all over." Herein lies the healing of memories.

2.   Confess Your Sin to God.

Unforgiveness is sin against God. It is disobedience to His command to forgive others even as God has forgiven us (see Eph. 4:32). Even more, God desires for all people to know forgiveness; He sent His Son, Jesus, to die to make that possible. Unforgiveness can stop people from experiencing God's forgiveness. Unforgiveness is a terrible sin against God.

Yet God is always ready to forgive those who call on Him (see Ps. 86:5). So accept your unforgiveness as sin, and confess it to God. Do you know what He does then?

"If we confess our sins, He is faithful and just to forgive us our sins and to cleanse us from all unrighteousness" (1 John 1:9 NKJV). This confessing implies naming our sins one by one.

"He who covers his sins will not prosper, but whoever confesses and forsakes them will have mercy" (Proverbs 28:13 NKJV).

How can we be sure we are forgiven? It's by God's Word! He very clearly says; "For if you forgive men their trespasses, your heavenly Father will also forgive you" (Matt. 6:14 NKJV).

Yet sometimes you still doubt that you are really forgiven. There is one more thing that you need to do. Receive God's forgiveness, accepting it just as you would accept a gift someone gave to you. How is this possible? Listen to what the apostle Paul said: "Now then, we are ambassadors for Christ, as though God were pleading through us; we implore you on Christ's behalf, be reconciled to God. For He made Him who knew no sin to be sin for us, that we might become the righteousness of God in Him" (2 Cor. 5:20-21 NKJV).

3.   Ask Forgiveness From Those You Wronged.

We are responsible to restore relationship with anyone who has anything against us (see Matt. 5:23-24). Accept responsibility for the wrong you have done, and ask for the person's forgiveness. If you do not know what you did wrong, ask God to show you.

Simply ask forgiveness. Do not go into details that would do more harm than good.

If you do not have a genuine sorrow or repentance in going to that person, stop first and prayerfully ask God to show you how you hurt that person and how he may have felt. Allow God to give you a whole new understanding and sensitivity toward that person.

It is good to look right at the person when you tell him what you did wrong and ask, "Will you forgive me?" Wait for an answer. If he says, "Yes, I will forgive," this will bring a release to him also. (Regardless of the answer, by confessing your sin and asking forgiveness, you have been obedient. You can now leave the situation in God's hands.)

4.   Ask God to Bless the Person Who Hurt You.

"Bless those who curse you, and pray for those who spitefully use you" (Luke 6:28 NKJV).

Ask God to truly bless the person who hurt you. And as you do this, follow the example of Jesus in asking God to bless him by forgiving him!

5.   Do Something Nice for the Person Who Hurt You (Bless Them).

"Do good to those who hate you" (Luke 6:27 NKJV).

"Do not be overcome by evil, but overcome evil with good" (Romans 12:21 NKJV).

This could be accomplished by complimenting that person, baking some cookies, fixing their car, or baby-sitting. Ask God, and He will show some act that will be meaningful to that person.

6.   Accept the Person the Way He or She Is, Even if He Is Wrong.

Don't defend what he does, but defend him. You do not necessarily need to approve of what he is doing, but treat him with dignity, respect, love, and kindness anyway.

"Therefore receive one another, just as Christ also received us, to the glory of God" (Romans 15:7 NKJV).

7.   Look at the Person Through the Eyes of Faith.

Do not concentrate on areas of weakness, sin, or irritation. Rather, concentrate on seeing that person as God wants him to be. Believe that God will answer your prayers for that person (see 1 John 5:14-15). Follow Abraham's example, and by faith see things that are not as they appear (see Rom. 4:16-21). Begin to think and speak positively about that person (see 1 Cor. 13:7). Love "believes all things, hopes all things."

Summary

Here is a short, personalized summary of these seven steps to forgiveness:

1. In Jesus' name, I choose to forgive those who have hurt me.
2. I will confess my sins to God, especially the terrible sin of unforgiveness. (And, by faith, I will receive God's forgiveness and cleansing.)
3. I will, as God directs me, ask others for forgiveness for the wrongs I have done to them. (And I will make restitution as needed.)
4. From now on, I will ask God to bless the one who has hurt me.
5. I, too, will bless that person, doing kind, helpful things for him.
6. I will accept him and treat him with love and respect.
7. I will look at that person through eyes of faith, and trust God to work in him.

List below any persons that you know you need to forgive. This list may include your spouse, a parent, a friend, a coworker, someone from your childhood, yourself, or perhaps even God.

Pray over this list individually or with your spouse and be accountable to your postmarital counselors. Be sure to look back over the seven steps and see if you have completed them for each person you need to forgive.

Closing Words of Encouragement

We want to thank you for persevering through the *Called Together* book and counseling process! You will be able to apply the material in the years ahead. We hope that you will remember the wise counsel you have received. Marriage is work, pure and simple, but is also one of the most rewarding life experiences. "Young" love is exciting and fun; "old" love is richly familiar and secure.

Hold hands. Touch one another. Share repeatedly how much you love and appreciate one another. Guard that which the Father has given the two of you, and never let anyone (including children) enter into the intimacies of this lifelong relationship. Becoming one is something you will do daily, not something you completed on your wedding day. Saying "I do" turns into saying, "I still do" each day of your life, even when you may not feel particularly close.

To work at a relationship means that you will put the needs of another before your own needs. That process, unlike our "me" centered culture, is the opposite of selfishness and self-centeredness. Seek counsel quickly when you have an issue causing ongoing disagreement. Admitting a problem and receiving godly counsel is more an act of maturity than hiding or covering up an issue in your marriage.

Prioritize getting away together for regular dates, weekend retreats, marriage seminars, and just "hanging out together," uninterrupted by anyone and anything. Pray for and with one another, and never lose this most intimate act of service. When you're apart, call and e-mail daily; send cards and flowers to celebrate important days and to simply celebrate life together. Write love notes, and purchase special little gifts for one another. Speak love, show love, write love, pray love, and provide loving touch.

We have discovered that change is constant in marriage. Sometimes it is planned change, and sometimes it is unexpected change. The latter can be the most challenging, but can also be the most exciting. When our lives are fully committed to our Lord, we can learn to trust Him completely, knowing that He is aware of everything in our lives. Trusting Him means that we will not have to figure it all out, but that we can walk with Him through the change and actually embrace what He may be bringing to us. While change may be constant, fear or insecurity does not need to be when we know our marriage is in His hands.

Last, we would like to speak a blessing over you and your marriage:

"Father, we ask that You will take this new marriage union beyond anything they could ask or imagine. As they walk with You, may they walk beside one another knowing Your hand is guiding them all the days of their life. We ask for an intimate relationship with You and out of that will flow an intimate relationship with one another. We declare blessing over them. In Jesus' name, Amen."

Endnotes

1. Norm Wright, *Training Christians to Counsel* (Eugene, OR: Harvest House, 1977).

2. This material was adapted from Wayne Mack's *A Homework Manual for Biblical Counseling, vol. 2* (Phillipsburg, NJ: Presbyterian and Reformed Pub., 1980).

3. Ibid.

Additional Wisdom Section

When Christians Remarry

It is not a secret that Christians remarry after the premature death of a spouse, after divorce, or when, as a senior, a life mate passes on into eternity. In each and every case, the problems and solutions are unique. These three sections, "Remarriage after the Death of a Spouse," "Remarriage after Divorce," and "Remarriage as Seniors," are written to effectively challenge and prepare you for entering into remarriage.

You will encounter Scriptures that will make you reflect upon your personal theology of remarriage. Every remarriage will affect numerous persons in your life. You must, with grace and an open heart and mind, face any and all challenges to arrive at the truth in God's Word. Remarriage, like any life-changing decision, must reach beyond emotions and find not *your* will, but *His* will to be done in your life and in the lives of those who are touched by this decision to remarry.

Remarriage After the Death of a Spouse

Perhaps no one really understands the almost physical pain that occurs when losing one's soul mate. Whether the marriage was one year long or 15 years in length, only those who have gone through it can speak to all the feelings and the recovery from such a huge loss.

After talking with those who have experienced such a tragedy, we have put into writing what prospective partners may experience when entering into a marriage after the death of a spouse.

They say that time heals, but what we heard was that it's not *time* as much as it is *distance* from a very traumatic event that brings healing, as well as the support from friends who stand faithfully by. That *distance* removes some of the sharp impact found within grief. The grief process is a God-given process and one that is vital to a healthy recovery from the loss. Children also help in the process, as they are the ones who remain from the lost love. They represent something that the former husband and wife brought into this world through their lives as one.

And now that oneness is challenged by separation from one's other half—a half that you had no idea could mean so much until it was gone.

By now, as you think of remarriage, the clothes and the shoes, the personal belongings like jewelry, the many pictures (not all of them), the special chair and the cosmetic items have been respectfully removed. It takes effort to accomplish each of these monumental tasks. You have had to enact many legal changes, each time having to announce your loss. Some areas can be avoided for months after the death of a spouse, but eventually, as health comes from recovery, these areas must be faced, and hard questions must be answered.

There can be vast differences in how quickly spouses leave this world. Jeff's wife, Lynda, was transported to the emergency room via ambulance after Jeff found her unconscious on their bedroom floor. Within three days she was gone. How could he have prepared himself for this? Laura's husband, John, died after a lengthy battle with cancer. One couple faced the possibility of death, and the other had no time to prepare. Neither situation would we wish upon anyone.

For the Christian, death is simply a key to open a door to Heaven. Jesus said He defeated death and that He is the resurrection and the life (see Rev. 1:18). Make no mistake: knowing this eases the pain but does not erase it. Having eternity together is certainly something to look forward to, but the presence of one's life partner is something to hold onto and not to be taken for granted. Through this loss, growth is forced like a green shoot from a bulb in the spring. One begins to discover that adversity and deep trials, if pushed through, force growth like no other time in life. One may also discover the great loss the Father endured by sending His Son to the cross. While painful, in time some of the "good" (as in, everything works together for the good...) surfaces. This forced growth can either cause one to be more aware of the pain of others or can keep one inwardly focused. It's an option that is our choice.

Where Are You With the Pain of the Loss?

How have you worked through all of the role changes and challenges? What steps have you taken in order to find a new identity in being single again? How have you grown spiritually and emotionally? Who can attest to your personal emotional health? How are your children coping? How much time has passed since the death of your spouse? Are your friends still present even though the meals and cards have stopped? How can you better identify with the Father's loss in sending His only Son? What new meaning has the promised resurrection taken on for you?

You have experienced going from being single to married and back to singleness again. However, this "singleness again" is a very different life. There may be many role changes, perhaps adapting to being both mother and father. A surprise to Jeff was to receive his first ever Mother's Day card as a single dad. When single again, identity becomes a huge issue. Jeff gave us some very insightful observations when he said, "I did not know who I was without Lynda." He went on to reveal, "I had to work through how I fit into life again, not even wanting to be on this earth at times. How you now relate to so many relationships from your former marriage is different from how you relate to those same persons as a single again—school teachers, neighbors, family, coworkers, and church friends. It all creates a new struggle for self-identity."

There are routines and habits from your former marriage, as well as deeply ingrained traditions. During singleness, these will be somewhat of a life-line, but when approaching remarriage, they become subjects for discussion. To assume you will keep all your former family traditions could be assuming too much and could be presuming upon this new relationship. You will have to discover what will be your new traditions and routines.

We heard that there are more questions through this time than there are answers. The "why" question is impossible to answer. But as the hope and expectation builds from the excitement of this new relationship, a new focus is born. At first, Jeff told us that he felt as though he was being unfaithful to his former spouse when considering another relationship. Then he said, "No, Lynda would want my life to go on, and she would want the children to have a wonderful mother again." Laura hesitantly told us, "I had made a decision to never marry again. John and I, being middle aged, were married a long time, and I knew no one could possibly replace him." And then she laughed and said, "It took me by surprise to find out that someone could not replace him, but could be a husband to me and not look like or sound like John. I had no idea that I could fall in love with someone who was not like my long-time friend and faithful marriage partner, and I can't tell you what joy it has brought to me."

Heart Change

It seems that this refocusing does not change the memories as such, but it does change something in the heart. There is the fresh excitement of a new love and the anticipation of future days that are mostly good, filled with family busyness and couple conversation. The reconnect with companionship is something longed for and now a close reality. "It is amazing what God has done…never in my wildest dreams could I have planned this…life is full of wonderful surprises, and this is one of them," were some of the many comments we have received.

At the same time, be prepared for some of the most unexpected sights or thoughts to bring a return of memories and emotions. One husband we talked to said just the sight of a yard sale brought back memories of his wife and how much she enjoyed yard sale shopping. At those moments, he found himself dealing with grief again. He advised, "Allow one another private times for grief, and do not feel as though you need to fix this grief or try to meet this other person's every need at the moment." You cannot fix another, and you cannot possibly be all they need; that is God's job.

Laura told us that it is good to look forward again instead of doing so much looking backward. Today she says that her remarriage with a new life partner is not without its challenges. There are huge adjustments after a season of independence. In this respect, remarriage for any reason calls for plenty of godly counsel, much prayer, and an openness to look at all the issues. With age comes wisdom, and with wisdom comes more grace. It is that all-important grace that any remarriage needs to lean upon.

Questions to Consider

1. How has your identity been challenged as you have gone from singleness to marriage, to singleness again?

2. What relationship do you now see yourself having with your former spouse's family, and how much will you and your new spouse relate with them?

3. How have you dealt with people who have wanted to shelter you (due to your loss) from problems they may see in your life or in the lives of your children?

4. With this new person in your life, how will you go from having all responsibility to sharing responsibility again?

5. How will you handle the "If I don't do it, it won't get done" syndrome?

6. You have had to step into new roles since the loss of your spouse. What roles do you prefer no longer to take responsibility for?

7. Have you given each other permission and freedom to talk about your departed spouse? Yes _____ No _____

8. How will I refer to my deceased wife/husband in present day conversation with my fiancé/ée?

9. Will my spouse change her last name when we marry?

10. What is the best way to deal with wedding photos from our prior marriage in our home? In the homes of our parents and former in-laws?

11. Describe how you find each other dealing with the need for security in this new relationship when conversations about your past relationship surface, while at the same time not feeling threatened?

12. What steps do you see yourself taking in order to face the fact that this new spouse/marriage will not be the same as your former spouse/marriage?

13. What steps will you take to identify comparison and not to compare this spouse/marriage to your former spouse/marriage?

14. How will you handle items remaining from your deceased spouse and possibly being a part of this new household?

15. What are some ways that you can support each other through "milestone" dates such as a birthday, former anniversary, Christmas, etc.?

16. Do you find your children desiring to live in the past, having a stronger focus on memory rather than a vision for the future? Yes _____ No _____
How will you help your children maintain good memories while at the same time fully entering into today and this new household?

17. What family traditions do you desire to bring into this marriage?

18. What steps can you take not to make this new spouse/marriage into one that looks like or feels like your former spouse/marriage?

19. How will we handle changes to our personal wills when we are married?

20. How will we plan for guardians for our children in our wills in the event of our deaths? Will the children remain together in a single household?

21. How should my children refer to my new wife's/husband's parents? Will we adopt our stepchildren?

22. Will the stepchildren's last name change? How will we handle legal custody of our stepchildren?

Additional Exercises

Persons experiencing this type of remarriage will also need to complete the following exercises found within the "Remarriage After Divorce" section:

"Children" (if applicable)

"Questions to Ask Your Children" (if applicable)

"Questions to Consider"

"Remarriage Interview"

"Progression of Healing"

Remarriage After Divorce

Divorce is absolutely the worst experience I've ever faced in my 53 years of life," Jim told me during a recent phone conversation. "It put my family through hell and back again. We'll never be the same."

Like a tape, I can hear Jim's words over and over again. Consider for a moment that Jim's experience is multiplied repeatedly throughout our country on a daily basis! Jim is thinking about remarriage after four years of reflecting upon a broken marriage and subsequent divorce. Jim said, "My children, three of whom are now grown, still have not recovered from their parents' divorce."

"What do you mean?" I asked.

"They haven't talked to their mother since discovering through the events of the divorce that she had an adulterous affair."

Four years after the event, Jim's children are still affected by his divorce. "I react to anyone who mentions the words separation or divorce," Jim says. "I challenge them to count the cost, the devastation, and to seek counseling. They are often only seeing the immediate relief of the problem and the pain and are not seeing the long-term effects of divorce."

Jim is not the only one who feels this way. After completing a study with couples both inside and outside of our local church, I discovered similar concerns. Surfacing repeatedly in the surveys were such issues as children, stepchildren, husband/wife roles, problems of the former marriage, forgiveness, in-laws, finances, and the church's stand on divorce and remarriage. These are some of the issues that relate to divorce.

Biblical Grounds

The first question for us to consider is this: "Do you have the freedom to remarry according to the Scriptures?" We live in a fallen world and are born with a fallen nature. Consequently, there are many unbiblical grounds for divorce—even in the church.

According to Scripture, marriage is a covenant. Through a spoken vow we made a covenant before God and before witnesses. If there were no sin in this world, there would likewise be no divorce. Divorce is the result of sin.

While the Bible clearly states that reconciliation is God's first choice (see 1 Cor. 7:12-14), there are two conditions in Scripture in which divorce was permitted, but certainly not required.

The first condition is that of marital unfaithfulness (see Matt. 5:31-32; 19:9). The second is in the case of a nonbeliever leaving the believing spouse (see 1 Cor. 7:15-16).

When Would Remarriage Be Prohibited?

God created marriage; therefore, when two people are joined together, whether they are Christians or non-Christians, it is before God. When non-Christians marry and then subsequently divorce, they can be in violation of the Scriptures just as a Christian can be.

If one divorces as a non-Christian and then remarries another as a Christian, one is still responsible for the consequences of the first marriage. According to Second Corinthians 5:17, we are not to live in condemnation to our former sin (life), but in no way does this verse, which is often quoted by the divorced, give one a license to enter into remarriage. The idea here is that when one who has committed a murder becomes a new man through his newly found faith, he remains accountable for his "former" life of sin, although he is forgiven.

Andrew Cornes, an English theologian, writes, "God's absolute will is experienced in Genesis...it is wrong to divorce. This will of God for marriage has never been modified or abrogated. However, since men do not live up to the will of God, a law is introduced which does not commend divorce or say that it has now become the will of God...but which regulates it."[1]

When would remarriage be prohibited? Simply stated, when there is a non-biblical divorce, remarriage is forbidden. Consequently, from our understanding of Scripture, if a marriage partner commits adultery and the marriage ends in divorce, then the person who has committed adultery, as the sinning partner, must choose to remain single (see Matt. 5:31-32) or else perpetuate his sin.

A second area is found in First Corinthians 7:10-11, where Paul was quoting from the teaching of Jesus. If people choose to leave a marriage where there is no biblical grounds for divorce, and against the desire of their spouse, they are, as well, choosing to remain single.[2]

When a divorce occurs based upon the desertion of a believing spouse, then the offended party or that partner who has not sinned is free to remarry (see 1 Cor. 7:15). Of course, in the case of the death of a spouse, the partner is free to remarry. The Old Testament Jewish practice held that if there was a right to divorce, there was a right to remarry. The New Testament teachings of Paul did not contradict this belief.

Jesus' personal stand is recorded in Mark 10:1-12 and Matthew 19:1-9. His response to the Pharisees when they questioned Him about divorce was, "What did Moses command you?" (Mark 10:3). He then made it clear in verses five through nine that divorce was not God's plan from the beginning.

Finally, regardless of the reasons for divorce, Scripture reveals in Deuteronomy 24:1-4 that if a partner has remarried, the union is permanently broken and that reconciliation is not to be pursued. The idea of breaking up another marriage to remarry is forbidden in Scripture.

Is the question of remarriage settled in your heart with God, His Word, your church leadership, and with yourself? Do not make a decision based on emotion or other people's opinions. Be sure that you are clear in your heart and have the peace of God. If you do not have God's peace, it is wrong to move ahead into remarriage. If both of you do not have full peace, do not try to convince each other of your opinion. You will only have regrets later. Allow each other to make his or her personal decision. God's Word on divorce and remarriage is clear as previously outlined. As believers, we must choose to obey His Word. Obedience to God is more important than our personal feelings (see John 14:21).

Divorce Statistics and History

Are the divorce statistics really as bad as have been reported for several decades? "Marriage as an institution is coming to an end" has been prophesied for years, but, as it turns out, the statistic which holds that one of every two marriages ends in divorce is incorrect. *The Youth Worker Journal* quotes a Harris poll that states, "Only one out of eight marriages will end in divorce. And in any one year, the overall rate of breakup is only two percent." Pollster Louis Harris said, "The long–touted notion that half of all marriages fail is one of the most specious pieces of statistical nonsense ever perpetrated in modern times."[3]

Where did the skewed figures come from? The 1981 report of the U.S. National Center for Health Statistics reported that there were 2.4 million new marriages and 1.2 million divorces that year. When that information was passed on, the most important element was frequently omitted: "A much, much bigger 54 million other marriages just keep flowing along like Old Man River." The American family is surviving.

According to the National Center for Health Statistics, the highest number of divorces takes place within the first five years of marriage. This is one reason why a pre- and postmarital mentoring relationship is so vital. An important distinction to make, however, is "new marriages" vs. "all marriages" when looking at statistical data.

Divorce Statistics Today

The most recent survey was conducted by George Barna. In his research, Barna surveyed 3,142 randomly selected adults and found that 24 percent of adults who have been married have also been divorced.[4] Barna further discovered that the divorce rate among born-again Christians was even higher (27 percent).

Barna concludes that a person's faith does not seem to have a major effect upon whether or not a person divorces. These statistics are certainly better than one in every two couples divorcing, but uncomfortably high, nonetheless. We believe that the biblical principles found within *Called Together* along with couple-to-couple mentoring can continue to battle this attack against God's institution of marriage.

God Can Identify With Divorce

How is it that God understands divorce so well? The answer: He has experienced divorce! In Jeremiah 3:2,6 we are told that Israel "defiled" the land through her "prostitution and wickedness." Israel committed adultery, and in verse eight, Jeremiah records, "I gave faithless Israel her certificate of divorce and sent her away because of all her adulteries...."

How much God loved Israel. He extended mercy to Israel over and over again. Now Israel's prostitution, her unfaithfulness, is more than He can bear. He will divorce Himself from such a sinful people, a people with no shame and no morals.

Have you experienced adultery committed against you? God understands. He knows how you feel because He has been there. Israel's immorality did not matter to her, and the consequence was a land that was defiled (see Jer. 3:9). Have you felt defiled by the adulterer or have you defiled another by committing adultery?

Listen to God's words in Jeremiah 3:12-14:

"Return, faithless Israel," declares the Lord, "I will frown on you no longer, for I am merciful," declares the Lord, "I will not be angry forever. Only acknowledge your guilt— you have rebelled against the Lord your God. You have scattered your favors to foreign gods under every spreading tree, and have not obeyed Me," declares the Lord. "Return, faithless people," declares the Lord, "for I am your husband. I will choose you...."

God cried out for Israel to return so He could show mercy and not remain angry because of their sins. He pleads for us to acknowledge our guilt. He then declares (paraphrased), "I can't divorce you. I'm still your husband; I choose you; I love you too much to let you go." If you are still dealing with guilt, acknowledge it, and choose to move on by accepting God's acceptance of you. God has called you to be free!

Trust

When a relationship is broken, trust disintegrates. Men and women who come through the other side of divorce often declare the curse-filled words, "I'll never trust again." It is understandable why these words might be spoken, but God had to move on and trust His people again, even after repeated adultery. If you do not deal with the trust issue, the small offenses in your next marriage may become exaggerated.

I recall a client who simply could not deal with her husband's sexual attraction to other women. To her, it represented a breach of their marriage vows, an unpardonable, unforgivable sin. Why such strong feelings? The answer was that adultery existed in her past, as well as in her former spouse's life. Now, as a newly married couple, their own experience with premarital sex added to their marital problems.

Where there is mistrust, one will often take things too personally. When your new partner comes home from work later than you were told, the situation can quickly be exaggerated. Have you effectively dealt with the mistrust issues?

Remarriage must not serve as a test to see if you have dealt with the mistrust issues. To trust again, you will need to work through your hurt feelings, repent of any bitterness or unforgiveness, and move to release and forgive your former spouse. The hurt from a prior marriage can deteriorate the foundation of a new marriage. You must choose to move to a new level of trust—one of trusting Jesus in the life of the one to whom you are relating.

Fear

Fear is the opposite of love. If satan can hold you in fear, he will keep you from truly experiencing love. When fear enters a relationship, love dissipates. Fear and love cannot abide in the same home or in the same relationship. If you fear someone, loving him or her will be an ongoing challenge.

"Love is patient, love is kind. It does not envy, it does not boast, it is not proud. It is not rude, it is not self-seeking, it is not easily angered, it keeps no record of wrongs," says First Corinthians 13:4-5. You cannot substitute the word fear for love in these Scriptures. Try it. It will not work because "[t]here is no fear in love. But perfect love drives out fear, because fear has to do with punishment. The one who fears is not made perfect in love" (1 John 4:18 NKJV).

Fear can play a major role in remarriage. If one marriage has failed, it certainly stands to reason that another could fail. This is fear. If one spouse has sinned, another could sin. Again, the motivation is fear. Just because someone says he is a Christian does not mean he will not change and become a different person (fear).

Does fear grip you? Then it is time to fall out of fellowship with fear and be renewed in Jesus' love. Remember the verse, "Perfect love drives out fear"? Take authority over fear in your life in Jesus' name. Drive it out by the power of the blood of Jesus, and put on His robe of love so you can be free from fear.

Fear can keep you from a wholehearted commitment to a new relationship. Having "broken" one vow, it is easy to think about breaking another. It is important to understand that there needs to be a solid commitment "for the remainder of our lives on this earth" to weather all the challenges that may be ahead.

If fear or mistrust tries to come between you and the one you love, share the thought or the feeling immediately. Do not allow it to fester in your mind. Satan will attempt to exaggerate that fear or mistrust. After you share, pray together. Drive the fear or the mistrust out with honesty, accountability, and prayer.

Reprogramming

Thomas J. Watson, the former president of IBM, once said to Arthur Gordon, a young writer, "You're making a common mistake. You're thinking of failure as the enemy of success. But it isn't at all. Failure is a teacher—a harsh one perhaps, but the best."[5]

How did you fail in your first marriage? Have you received personal counseling to help you admit your failures, talk them through, repent, and develop new and redeemed life patterns? If not, you will see these failures repeated. If you failed at communication, what have you learned? If you failed at role responsibility, how do you see roles differently? The bottom line is that you must take an honest and deep look at yourself.

Failure to do this keeps you in denial and blame. The result will be no spiritual or emotional growth and maturity on your part.

The number one reason for failure of marriages is selfishness—we want what we want (see James 3:13-18; 4:1-3). Have you matured beyond this? Can you remove the shaded glasses of mistrust, immaturity, guilt, rejection, and selfishness from your eyes?

Can you put on the life of Christ who came in the form of a servant? "Who, being in very nature God, did not consider equality with God something to be grasped, but made Himself nothing, taking the very nature of a servant, being made in human likeness" (Philippians 2:6-7).

Can you reprogram that old way of thinking about marriage, about sex, about money, about your needs? It is vital to confront these old patterns of thinking. Romans 12:2 says that we are to be "transformed by the renewing of [our] mind." Have you sincerely asked the Lord to expose wrong thinking from past relationships? I encourage you to stop and do this now.

Write down some of those misbeliefs (wrong thoughts) you've brought with you from your former marriage. As you record them, ask the Lord to reveal the truth of Scripture to replace the wrong thinking. Review the "Knowing Who You

Are in Christ" worksheet found in Session One of *Called Together*. Renew your mind with truth, not the lies from the past.[6]

Children and Stepchildren

How do you love a child who is not your own? Will this child accept you? If both of you are bringing children into a new marriage union, how will they get along? The subject of children was the most talked about topic in our surveys with remarried couples. The unanticipated adjustments for the children and their parent who was remarrying provoked the most problems for these couples.

The *Divorce Recovery Workbook* lists three reasons for this difficult transition:[7] In the children's minds…

1. It ends the fantasy that their parents might get back together.
2. It triggers the fear that the new spouse will take away the love their parent has for them.
3. It creates anxiety about whether they will get along with this intruder in their family.

Children need time to heal from a divorce. Their own feelings of hurt, rejection, separation anxiety, fear, and anger must be talked about. If this outlet of healing is not provided, parents will find tension and strife in their relationship with their child.

It will take time to bond with stepchildren. Older children can be very resistant to this process. They feel the loss of a parent more than they feel the excitement of having a new parent. It is strongly advised that the children enter the process of premarital counseling. This will help them deal with some of these issues before a remarriage takes place.

Allow the children time to accept the changes forthcoming and to develop a relationship with the stepparent. Don't expect immediate acceptance. Ask what the children prefer to call the stepparent. Be prepared to be rejected. Do not retaliate with rejection on your part.

Never try to compete with the ex-spouse's relationship with his or her child. This will not impress the stepchild, and may cause even more distance. As they sense their parent's loyalty moving toward a stepparent-to-be, their communication may decrease. Individual counseling for the children may be advisable.

Along with the emotions listed above, here are some topics to consider addressing with children in premarital counseling: discipline (old/new rules), parental roles, parental authority, visitation, and changes in such areas as school, residence, bedroom arrangements, sports, jobs, and finances.

No matter how fairly you try to treat your children, you will most likely see your children, your spouse's children, and any children born to this new union differently. Although you may have the same goal for all of the children, the way you treat each one will take tremendous grace. This grace will allow Christ-centered blended families to experience happiness and unity.

Maintain Your Focus

In American society today, the family focus has become the children. This should not be the case. The focus needs to be the marriage. A child-centered focus disrupts marital unity and agreement. The marriage will need to be stable and healthy after the children have left home. Many couples do not have a relationship left after the children are raised because their marriage focus was out of balance.

Children (especially children from blended families) need security. Security, however, does not come from purchasing lots of material things (electronic gadgets, computers, cars, etc.). Security does not come from our children attending every extracurricular school activity or every friend's party. Security for children is a product of Mom and Dad loving each other and prioritizing God's principles in their marriage. Ask any child: Would you prefer that Mom and Dad stay married and work on their relationship, or would you like the newest, the best, the most expensive _____? Children want their parents to stay together.

Goals and Vision

Why are you considering remarriage? Why this person? What is the goal, the vision of this marriage? Are you considering remarriage for the sake of convenience, for providing a parent to your children, for financial help, to take care of loneliness, or just because you want to remarry? These are not reasons for remarriage.

Marriage is for the mature. Only mature people can maintain a lifetime commitment. Marriage changes a person's status, not the person. Are you overlooking something in each other's lives that you think will change when you marry? Are you compromising on your personal standards in any way by considering this person? If the answer is "yes" to either question, you are involved in immature thinking and are not facing reality.

If your answer is "no," then move on to this question: Why is God calling us together? What is His goal/vision for us? What is it in this vision that we can only fulfill by becoming married? You must discover His answer to these questions.

Other Areas to Consider

One couple interviewed said that they had made a big mistake by moving into "his house with his daughters." Given the chance to do it over again, they would have sold both properties and moved into a new, neutral home. There are memories and loyalties connected to homes, and this potential problem could be resolved by relocating to a new property.

If you have been without a spouse for some time, please consider that you will be giving up your independence. You will be going back to making cooperative decisions and being involved in mutual submission. You will need to reconsider some of your independent patterns of living.

Consider your former in-laws, as well as future in-laws. What will the relationships be like? How will they change? What will be decided in regards to grandchildren and visitation?

What church will you attend? Will people in your church find it difficult to see you with another spouse? Will you need to consider attending a new church and developing new relationships?

Have you discussed your financial obligations? Are you aware of each other's indebtedness? Are you ready to assume this indebtedness? Have you communicated about your savings, retirement plans, life insurances, checking accounts, and credit accounts?

Are you reading books on the topics of divorce and remarriage, children of divorced parents, and other related topics? See the recommended reading list in this section. You can learn so much from other people's experiences.

Have you given yourself sufficient time to grieve the loss of a marriage? Some experts believe that no one should begin to consider remarriage after divorce or the death of a spouse within one year after the loss. Others extend that time period to two years. This all-important time factor allows you to go through the healing process, as well as the adjustments. If you have children, they need this time to adjust as well. If a new relationship begins too soon, the children will often automatically reject the person seeing their mom or dad.

This is not just a "get over it" or a "get back to everyday normal life" time period. It is a time to discover what "normal" is. It is also a time to work through the emotions. This event sends shock waves to the core of your being. You must allow sufficient time for healing and adjusting.

Finally, consider becoming a team again. Reflect on how you see a marriage team operating. How would it differ from how your first marriage operated? One couple shared with me that they began their remarriage with a competitive spirit rather than a team spirit. They needed to deal with their self-pride, their jealousy of one another, their differences in handling the children, and the decision regarding which one of them would cook the meals. As they dealt with these areas, the competitive spirit gave way to a team spirit. Eventually they developed their own cooperative way which was unique to them as a newly married couple.

The Final Word: Forgiveness

Jesus said, "For if you forgive men when they sin against you, your heavenly Father will also forgive you. But if you do not forgive men their sins, your Father will not forgive your sins" (Matthew 6:14-15).

Are you unforgiving toward God, your former spouse, former in–laws, former friends, a pastor or Sunday school teacher, or yourself? If the slate is not clean, you will infect this new marriage relationship with your unwillingness to forgive.

Forgiveness is not saying that your former spouse was right. Forgiveness is letting go of the many hurts and wounds inflicted by that person so you can be healed. The healthier you are, the healthier your marriage will be. Forgiveness also means being reconciled to your former spouse in order to interact with him/her over the myriad of children's issues.

Being unwilling to forgive spreads like cancer and is deadly. Forgiveness is the last stage of divorce recovery and the first stage of a new view of life. It is saying good-bye to the denial, the shock, the anger, the depression, the fear, and the rejection.

Forgiveness brings you into a new realm of acceptance and wholeness. Forgiving is Jesus' medicine. It comes straight from the cross. It is the blood that poured from the veins of God. It is the "Jesus factor."

Consider praying this prayer with us:

Dear heavenly Father,

Thank You for experiencing divorce for me and with me. Thank You for going through the pain and the rejection of separation and divorce. Thank You for Your grace that has brought me to this place in my life. At times, I may have even felt rejected by You. I was not. At times, I thought I bore this pain alone. I did not. And at times, I thought my anger would change our relationship forever. My relationship with You is more secure today. You have seen me through so much. While I may walk "with a limp," it is a reminder of my inabilities and of Your abilities.

Forgive me now for holding anything against anyone. I release _____ [insert specific name(s)] in Jesus' name and commit them to You. I place them into Your hands. I thank You, Father, that the shed blood of Jesus covers my sin, as well as their sin. I declare freedom from bitterness or any lingering effects of being unwilling to forgive. Renew my mind and my heart.

In Jesus' name, Amen.

As you have taken a step of faith by forgiving and releasing hurts from the past, know that freedom will come to have trust increase and fear decrease. God's best to you on your remarriage journey.

Endnotes

1. Andrew Cornes, *Divorce and Remarriage: Biblical Principles and Pastoral Practice* (London: Hodder & Stoughton, 1993).

2. The New Testament verses on divorce and remarriage are as follows: Matthew 5:31–32; Matthew 19:1–12; Mark 10:1–12; Luke 16:18; 1 Corinthians 7:10–16.

3. Youth Worker Journal 2, no. 1 (September 1987).

4. Jim Killam, "Don't Believe the Divorce Statistics," *Partnership* (Summer 1997). See also the most recent statistics regarding marriage and divorce released by the Barna Group (March 31, 2008) at http://www.barna.org/FlexPage.aspx?Page=BarnaUpdateNarrow&BarnaUpdateID=295.

5. Arthur Gordon, *A Touch of Wonder* (New York, NY: Jove Books, 1986).

6. For more in-depth focus on renewing your mind, see William Backus, *Learning to Tell Myself the Truth: A Six Week Guide* (Minneapolis, MN: Bethany House Publishers, 1994).

7. Bob Burns and Tom Whiteman, *The Fresh Start Divorce Recovery Workbook* (Nashville, TN: Oliver Nelson, 1992). A seminar and workbook of 300 pages that will help you face the past, the present, and the future concerning divorce.

History Questionnaire

Because couples bring their history with them, it is important for each of you to know whether or not you have dealt with the issues of the past. Complete the following exercise individually.

1. Discuss some of the mistakes you made in your previous marriage relationship.

2. What have you done to work on the areas you wrote about in number one?

3. How can you demonstrate the healing you have received from past experiences and hurts? To what evidence can you point to show new patterns in current relationships?

4. How long have you lived without a spouse? With what areas of independence do you believe you may struggle if you remarry?

5. Were there any experiences of abuse from your previous marriage, and, if so, what were they?

6. Since experiencing this abuse, what have you come to believe about it?

7. According to Matthew 7:3 (looking at the fault in your brother's eye and not considering your own), how will you handle the temptation to express in a negative manner something that you see in your mate that existed in your former spouse?

8. What interaction will you have with your former spouse?

9. Does your future spouse have a workable relationship with his/her former spouse?

10. What will you consider reasonable interaction for your spouse to have with his/her former spouse?

11. Because of a previous marriage ending in divorce, how will you handle feelings of insecurity when going through a difficult time with your new spouse?

12. In your previous marriage, did you find yourself providing any type of "cover up" for your spouse? Yes _____ No _____
    If yes, please expound.

13. As you consider spousal roles, what previous roles did you play that you do not desire to play in a new marriage? (For example, total caretaker of the finances, the children, etc.)

14. What were some of the expectations that you had of your former spouse that were not fulfilled?

15. What mistakes do you feel your former spouse made in marriage?

16. For what things have you had to forgive your former spouse? Are there any areas of forgiveness that you still struggle with?

17. Have you discovered what kind of person you were married to and why you chose him or her? In other words, can you identify any wrong thinking patterns from the previous relationship?

18. What good thing(s) from your previous marriage relationship do you desire to bring into this new relationship?_____

Biblical Grounds

In the following exercise, please provide your personal scriptural response.

1. Upon what biblical grounds did you base your divorce? Name specific Scriptures and your interpretation of those verses.

2. Upon what biblical grounds do you base your remarriage? Specifically, what Scriptures do you use to back up your decision to remarry?

3. Discuss how you know you have God's peace and confirmation of this relationship.

4. Have you sought God's forgiveness for your part in the breakup of your former marriage relationship? Have you accepted that forgiveness?

5. What do you desire to accomplish by bringing two families together in remarriage?

Trust and Fear

Because trust and fear are two specific areas that affect couples who remarry, respond to the following questions individually.

1. What areas of trust were fractured in your previous marriage?
2. How has the Lord walked you through healing of this brokenness?
3. List any fears you have as you consider remarriage.
4. What steps will you take not to carry mistrust and fear into this new union? What action will you take if mistrust or fear becomes an issue?

Children

Divorce and remarriage are difficult for children. As you consider remarriage, think about how it will impact them. Respond individually to this exercise.

1. Have your children worked through the grief and/or rejection that can occur from divorce? Yes _____ No_____

2. What is their understanding of the broken relationship at this point of their lives?

3. Do your children blame themselves for any aspect of the divorce? Yes _____ No _____

4. Have your children made room in their heart for a stepparent? Yes _____No _____

5. What do you see as the best method to unite two families as one?

6. Discuss how you will love a child that is not your biological child.

7. Of the two of you, who do you believe is more strict when it comes to parenting?

8. Will you allow one another to correct any child freely? Yes _____ No _____

9. Who do you see as responsible to provide the primary discipline of the children?

10. Do you feel it is necessary for your stepchildren to follow the rules you have made for your own biological children? Yes _____ No _____ Name any examples that you can think of where this would not be the case.

11. Finish this sentence: Accepting my future spouse's children into our home and our family will be...

12. Please list your methods of discipline along with sample offenses.

13. What are some of your goals for your children and stepchildren?

14. What are some practical ways you can guard against jealousy that your children may feel toward your new partner?

15. Will you have children together in this new union? Yes _____ No _____ How many? _____

16. How will you handle a stepchild rejecting you?

17. What name do you expect the stepchildren to call you?

18. How do you see bonding taking place with stepchildren?

19. Have you met the former wife/husband of your future spouse? How do you view his/her parenting skills?

20. Do you both agree with the visitation arrangements of noncustodial children? Yes _____ No _____

21. Does your potential spouse understand and agree with any financial commitments you have concerning child support?
    Yes _____ No _____

22. Will any of your children (biological or stepchildren) need to change schools, jobs, churches, activities, or move away from friends or grandparents? Yes _____ No _____ How will you handle this?

23. Have you discussed with the children a new place of residence, bedroom arrangements, and/or the sharing of toys?

24. How will you take financial responsibility for your stepchildren, even if this parent is receiving support?

25. Discuss with one another how you will handle the holiday season (gifts, grandparents, visitation, etc.).

26. You both are choosing to make the necessary changes for this new union. Your children, however, may not feel as though they have a choice. What will you do if your child feels "forced" into this decision with very little knowledge as to what this will mean for him/her and his/her future?

Questions to Ask Your Children

1.   What are some of the things you like or appreciate about your mother's or father's future spouse?

2.   Finish this sentence: When my mother/father remarries, I...

3.   One thing I fear about my parent remarrying is...

4.   An area that I am excited about concerning remarriage is...

5.   If you will be moving to another home, how do you feel about this?

6.   What are some of the changes you will need to face with a possible remarriage?

7.   Do you feel you are able to communicate well with your future stepparent?

8.   What do you desire to call your stepmother/stepfather?

9.   How do you get along with your future stepparent's children?

10. What are your thoughts about your future stepparent administering discipline to you?

11. What will you do when you do not agree with your stepparent?

12. Do you feel jealous about anything relating to this remarriage (for example, jealousy of a future stepbrother or sister, jealousy of someone trying to take your biological parent's place)?

13. Do you feel resentful about anything related to this remarriage (for example, resentment toward a future stepparent, resentment toward your parent for divorcing and entering this new relationship)?

14. Have you ever felt "demoted" by your parent because he or she was pursuing another marriage relationship?

15. Have you made room in your heart to receive a stepparent?

16. Have you felt free to express your feelings about your mother or father's decision to remarry?

17. Is there anything else you would like to share?

Other Questions to Consider

You may confer with one another as you respond to the following questions.

1. What church will you attend?
2. Where will you live?
3. How will you handle your savings accounts, retirements, and indebtedness?
4. What problems do you feel you still need to work through in this relationship before remarriage?
5. How are your fiancé/ée's character traits different from your former spouse's character traits?
6. Are these the character qualities that you have been looking for?
7. Do you anticipate any former or future in-law difficulties? Please expound.
8. Is there anyone questioning whether you should remarry at this time or enter into marriage with this person?
9. Where does your pastor and/or spiritual leader(s) stand as you consider remarriage?
10. Are there doubts or questions keeping you from being confident about your remarriage, and are you convinced that you are to marry this person?

Remarriage Interview

In this exercise you are requested to locate a couple who are remarried and ask them if they would be willing to communicate with both of you about some of the experiences they have had. The following are suggested questions you can ask to generate dialogue between you as couples.

1. Could you share with us some of the positive experiences you have enjoyed as a remarried couple?
2. What are some of the negative experiences you have encountered?
3. What keeps your marriage strong in the midst of differences?
4. What, if any, were areas of surprise to both of you?
5. If you brought children into this new union, what were your experiences with this blending?
6. How have you handled changes with church, finances, in-laws, friends, relocation, and other similar issues?
7. Now that you can look at your decision in retrospect, what would you have done differently, if anything?
8. How do you handle the temptation of mentioning your former spouse or of speaking negatively of your spouse's former mate?
9. How did you handle a "competitive spirit" and become a team?
10. What books have been helpful to you?

Scenario Response

Complete this exercise individually.

1. Your spouse has just corrected "your" child in a different way than he/she corrects "his/her" child. How will you handle this?

2. Something your spouse just did or said caused an emotion producing a flashback of your former spouse. What will you do?

3. You just tried to joke with your spouse, and he/she took offense because it reminded him/her of his/her former spouse. Your response might be...

4. You are noticing some distance between you and your stepchild. You ask him about it, and his reply is that there are no problems. What will your next step be?

5. You both are choosing to make the necessary changes for this new union. Stepchildren may not have the same option or choice. How will you handle children who feel "forced" to blend their families with very little knowledge and experience as to what this will mean for them and their future?

Progression of Healing

Before completing the "Progress of Healing" exercise, perhaps a bit of explanation is necessary. The purpose of this exercise is to provide a very important aspect of the remarriage process. Before you rent an apartment, buy a home, take in a foster child, or change jobs, often a "background check" is required. Someone takes an objective look at your history of payment or personal integrity. If you have been totally honest about your past, any check on your history is not threatening.

If your credit history is important to a loan officer, one with whom you will not have an ongoing relationship, how much more important is your progression of healing to the one with whom you desire to spend the rest of your life? Too many times couples have gotten into trouble with an "I love him; the past is the past" attitude which later turned devastatingly sour when "secrets" were exposed. Be honest, open, and willing to discover things about each other that will provoke further growth in your life.

In order for both of you to discover how you have progressed in the healing process, please list three names of contact persons. Preferably, these persons have walked through your divorce with you and can objectively attest to your personal healing process and recovery.

List names, addresses, and phone numbers of persons to contact:

Name

Address

Phone Number

Things I discovered about my future spouse and myself through this process:

Recommended Reading

Barnes, Robert. *You're Not My Daddy*. Dallas, TX: Word Publishers, 1992 (Out of Print).

Brown, Beth. *When You're Mom No. 2*. Ann Arbor, MI: Servant Publications, 1991 (Out of Print).

Deal, Ron. *The Smart Stepfamily*. Grand Rapids, MI: Bethany House, 2002, 2006.

Frydenger, Tom and Adrienne Frydenger. *Resolving Conflict in the Blended Family*. Tarrytown, NY: Chosen Books, 1987.

Lehman, Kevin. *Living in a Step Family Without Getting Stepped On*. Nashville, TN: Thomas Nelson, 1994.

Smoke, Jim. *Growing in Remarriage*. Old Tappan, NJ: Fleming H. Revell, 1990.

Remarriage as Seniors

The fastest growing segment of population in the United States today is the group known as "senior citizens," and almost half of women over age 65 are widows, according to the U.S. Census Bureau. Nearly 700,000 women lose their husbands each year.

Most seniors expect to enjoy life during retirement, maintain reasonably good health, and have a lifelong partner at their side. But what happens when that partner has preceded the other spouse to eternity? How does one deal with loneliness? Is it right to consider remarriage? Will the remaining spouse ever be happy again? Is it possible to feel excited about someone of the opposite sex and not feel guilty?

Sam and Helen had already experienced 58 combined years of marriage before their spouses died. Helen said that people wanted her to get on with her life quickly. Comments like, "Isn't there anybody good enough for you?" only caused her to feel condemned, unable to meet the expectations of those around her. Helen eventually sold her home and moved in with her son and daughter-in-law. Meanwhile in a neighboring town, Sam was allowing one of his four adult daughters to move into his home with her new husband. "We can help you, Dad, with the loss of Mom—and pay your rent," they said.

When Sam and Helen moved on from their grief and loss, they found each other. Both were finishing up teaching careers and neither of them had been desirous of joining the "dating scene." Although both knew the pain of loneliness, neither Sam nor Helen was willing to consider remarriage. Armed with their strong faith, Sam and Helen both depended on God to meet their emotional needs.

But God chose to meet those needs by bringing them together in marriage. Today, at the age of 64, after eight years of marriage, they are no longer lonely and rejoice that they could find happiness and fulfillment with a new spouse.

What were some of the obstacles along the way for this precious couple? Before you work through the questions in the exercises that follow, let us give you some background through the lives of Sam and Helen. Perhaps you'll identify with some of their thoughts.

Losses

Sam and Helen offer examples of some of the losses that are encountered when walking through the bereavement of a spouse. The intimacy one has had with a lifelong partner is beyond description. So much in this area can be taken for granted (for example, sharing secrets, having a deep familiarization with one person, the small acts of service, the security represented by this partner, personal gifts, and just having someone at your side).

These thoughts can perhaps be summed up in one word—*companionship*. Webster calls it a "matched pair or set." The loss of companionship affects us more deeply than lost financial resources or anything material. Jesus referred to the deep void one feels in lost companionship when He cried out from the cross, "My God, My God, why have you forsaken Me?" (Mark 15:34).

Have you effectively worked through your losses? Do you still hurt? Are you angry at God, others, or yourself? Do you feel any guilt from your former marriage? Dialogue with Jesus about these things and ask Him for healing.

Adult Children

Sam and Helen knew their relationship would cause adjustments when relating to their grown children. Even though the children said that they were "all for" their parents' newfound love relationship, many changes would be forthcoming.

After the loss of one parent, an adult child can have difficultly seeing his or her mother or father grow close to someone of the opposite sex. The parent desires to share their feelings of excitement with their children, but is not sure if their adult children want to hear about them. Helen said that it is "kind of a role reversal. Your children ask if you have held hands yet, or if you have kissed. It is uncomfortable for them." In one sense, they want to know in order to share their parent's joy. In another sense, however, they would rather not know the details.

One daughter felt like her father was moving too quickly. Sam and Helen's response was, "Why prolong the process? We both knew what we wanted and felt God's blessing upon our desires."

Another area to be dealt with was that of family heirlooms. Sam gave all of his former wife's heirlooms to his daughters. "After all," Sam said, "Helen and I didn't need them, and this way they needed to have no fear that they wouldn't receive these items in the future."

An adjustment in relationships will also be necessary. When Helen decided to remarry, the son with whom she was living began to experience feelings of loss—Mom would no longer live in his home. Helen and her daughter-in-law were very close; the living arrangement prior to remarriage had worked well. Her daughter-in-law said, "I feel like I'm losing my best friend." Today, however, most widows and widowers prefer to live on their own simply because they do not want to be a "burden" to their family.

Finances

Sam and Helen offer financial advice for those who are remarrying: be open and honest from the beginning. Do not separate finances, but bring finances together. In order to have this union succeed, a couple needs to have financial unity and move away from a "his and hers" mentality.

Some seniors are choosing to live together and remain unmarried based solely upon financial reasons. These persons do not desire to alter their retirement benefits or Social Security status. Even if a couple claims a platonic relationship, the appearance is a concern. Listen to the following verses found in First Thessalonians 5:21-22: "Test everything. Hold on to the good. Avoid every kind of evil." (Or "the appearance of evil," some texts read.) We are admonished to avoid anything that is questionable or could be seen as wrongdoing.

In addition, First Timothy 6:10 informs us, "...Some people, eager for money, have wandered from the faith and pierced themselves with many griefs." While you may not be "eager for money," basing your decision on financial income rather than faith in God's ability to supply all of our needs (see Phil. 4:11-13,19) is an act of trusting self more than God. God is a better provider than the government or any retirement plan.

Sharing Memories

Sam and Helen recommend to seniors who are serious about remarriage that they talk about their former spouse during their first weeks of courting.

"We spent a lot of time sharing about our first love," Helen said.

These were not conversations full of comparison, Sam said—just "letting it all out with someone who understood the experience."

"We recognized that when we shared all that we needed to share," Helen said, "we could then move on to other important areas of getting to know one another."

Sam and Helen made a promise to one another that they would not be involved in comparison during their courtship or throughout their marriage.

As you work through the exercises that follow, allow the Holy Spirit to point out and impress within you any areas where there is still confusion, hurt, loneliness, or loss. Our Father is such a Redeemer. Be open for prayer and input from your premarital counselors.

Questions to Consider

Complete this exercise individually.

1. Some adult children feel that Dad or Mom have their courtship in "overdrive." Have any of your children expressed this?
   Yes ____No _____

2. Do your adult children desire to hear about your dates, or do they avoid the subject?

3. Have you discovered any form of "role reversal" with your adult children? In other words, are they "checking up" on you and your future spouse's relationship? If so, has this been a problem or a blessing?

4. What do you desire your future step-grandchildren to call you?

5. Have you discussed family heirlooms? Do you both plan to keep, sell, or give away family heirlooms?

6. There can be a loyalty issue with possessions (furniture, etc.). Have you taken the time to discuss personal possessions? If so, what have you decided?

7. There are aspects of life that are "set in concrete." What are some of the areas you consider non-negotiable?

8. How will you leave independence and create a spirit of interdependence?

9. What church will you attend?

10. Where will you live?

11. How will you handle your savings accounts, retirement accounts, and any indebtedness?

12. Where does your pastor and/or spiritual leader(s) stand as you consider remarriage?

13. Are your parents still living? Have they given you any advice concerning remarriage? Yes _____ No _____
What was the advice?

14. How long have you lived without a life partner? What do you foresee as your most difficult adjustment?

15. When seniors consider remarriage, dreams about their departed life partner sometimes increase. How will you deal with this?

16. As you consider spousal roles once again, what previous roles did you play that you do not wish to repeat in a new marriage?

17. Did you have any expectations that were not fulfilled in your first marriage? Yes _____ No _____
What were they?

18. What good thing(s) from your previous marriage do you desire to bring into this new union?

19. If you are presently living in a retirement home, have you researched the policies concerning residents and marriage?

20. What will you gain by transitioning from dating to marriage? What are some losses that you would experience?

21. Have you discussed wedding plans? Yes _____ No _____
How do they differ from first-time weddings?

22. Have you discussed sexual attraction? Yes _____ No _____
What part will sex play in your marriage?
Have you discussed sexual impotency? Yes _____ No _____
23. What fears, if any, are you feeling about remarriage?
24. Are you presently experiencing any feelings of disloyalty to your former spouse? Yes _____ No _____
If yes, please expound.
25. Have you effectively worked through your loss of a life partner? Some of those losses are deep familiarization with another, oneness, mutual friendships, a parent of your children, and finances.

Loneliness

Complete this exercise individually.

1.   Describe the difference between "aloneness" and "loneliness." How have you experienced both of these?
2.   Where is God when one is experiencing loneliness?
3.   Describe the benefits of loneliness.
4.   How can loneliness serve as a life discipline?
5.   What have you discovered about yourself in loneliness?
6.   Does your "single identity" cause you to feel lonely? Please expound.
7.   How does Psalm 139:1-12 speak to your loneliness?
8.   Are you considering marriage as an escape from loneliness?

Scenarios

Complete this exercise individually.

1. Within the first year of remarriage, your new partner suffers a debilitating illness. How will you handle this unexpected condition?

2. Two years into your new marriage, certain family members are still upset that you remarried. How will you confront this disappointment?

3. You can't help but feel as though your new husband/wife has a strong desire to have you be like his/her former spouse. How will you respond?

4. Keeping in contact with both extended families has become increasingly difficult. What steps can you take to remedy the situation?

Intercultural and Interracial Marriages

Called Together does not shy away from what might be considered controversial marriages. Both interracial and intercultural marriages are occurring with more frequency in today's world. People are far more mobile. The Internet has brought worldwide relational connections.

Many nations are "melting pots" of culture. This brings another race or another culture to your town, your workplace, and to your college. Urban areas offer even more opportunities to experience cross-cultural relationships.

There are special considerations with each of these marriages. These two sections, "Intercultural Marriages" and "Interracial Marriages," provide for effective dialogue and offer questions to consider.

Intercultural Marriages

Intercultural marriages bring an extra set of dynamics to relationships. Many Christians leave their country of origin either for short-term or long-term missions, education, employment, or travel. In addition, many diverse cultures live together in the same country or city. Your neighbor may be from another culture.

Regardless how persons of differing cultures met and grew to love one another, the desire to marry calls for a merge of two cultures into one. Many questions may arise.

Will our families understand? What about spousal roles? What differences will be encountered with food and meal preparation? In which culture will we live? Which language will our children speak?

We created a survey questionnaire about intercultural marriage and asked many such couples to respond to some of the positives and negatives within an intercultural marriage. The answers were eye-opening and helpful.

First, we will discuss assumptions that are typically made within an intercultural relationship. Exercises touching on differences and communication challenges will follow.

Assumptions: My Way—the Right Way?

Probably one of the biggest assumptions made within marriage is that we assume the way we do things is the correct way. We think, "My family has always done it this way, and it works quite well." While this same assumption can be found within intercultural marriages, it tends to be magnified.

Assumptions about how we live come with each culture. All of our life experiences through family and cultural background teach us how to deal with life's challenges. Within an intercultural marriage, many different assumptions will surface over time. We will formulate our opinions and make judgments based upon our world view.

For example, there are banks in the United States, and there are banks in New Zealand. Both banks serve a similar function. In New Zealand checks do not have to be signed to be cashed. Deposit slips are completed very differently. In the United States, one banking company will not cash another's check unless you have an account with them. In New Zealand, the banks tend to work together. Neither banking system is wrong; however, to the spouse encountering a new and unfamiliar system, it may be a challenge. The tendency to think, "The way we did it in my country was better," may emerge.

Another difference to consider is the medical arena. Medical services differ greatly from country to country. One country may have social medicine, while other countries have very few doctors and distant or poor services. The United States has medical technology that many countries do not have, but has a higher cost and a system that requires individuals to pay their own bills instead of having government coverage. Will this present a problem for you? Consider this important medical question: Where will your children be born, and how will you arrive at this decision?

Other assumptions may be made in such areas as home decorating, the way money is handled, unfamiliar types of entertainment, differing degrees of acceptable openness in personal sharing, different understandings of extended family relationships, the celebration of unfamiliar holidays, differing views of romance, the use of free time and vacations, and the way children are educated. These areas are not meant to be all inclusive, but to give you a general idea about the assumptions we all have made and would need to face in the event of an intercultural marriage.

Some of the negatives discovered by couples who are interculturally married can be quite varied. One wife confessed that her way of doing certain things drew a negative response from her spouse (how dishes were washed, the care of clothing, or how the children were disciplined). Marrying someone from an underdeveloped country and then bringing that person to the United States may be shocking. The prosperity of North America can be incomprehensible. Likewise, the lack of what others may view as essentials can be equally shocking.

Adjusting to Differing Cultural Norms

Feeling as though you are expected to be like the wives or husbands of the culture you married into can be a monumental hurdle to cross. Cultural and social norms may be so diametrically opposed to those of your country of origin that you become emotionally confused. An inability to understand the perceived role is difficult enough. You may not agree with the traditions of the new culture you are living in.

Keep in mind that in some countries, it is acceptable for the man to marry outside his culture, but not for the woman—or vice–versa. This fact may make it more difficult to have a successful intercultural marriage in that particular country.

Caution One: Know Each Other's Culture!

With each of the couples we interviewed, several cautions emerged. One of the strongest was the need to become familiar with each other's culture. If at all possible, spend some time living in that culture before marriage. The minimum amount of time suggested was two to three months. While visiting your future spouse's country of origin, it would be important to live with a local family, as well as his/her family. This would enable you to experience firsthand the relationship differences within the family.

A word of caution: While you are picking up certain nuances, don't think that all families of this culture operate this way. It would be like saying all North American or European families function in a similar way.

So much can and should be learned about your future mate's culture before marriage. A wife shared with me that she never understood her husband's concept of time until she traveled to his country. "To my husband's culture, a moment may mean several hours," she explained. She went on to say that a wedding scheduled for 10:00 A.M. may begin at noon.

Imagine the challenges this one concept can present. When asked how she worked this problem out, she said, "My husband learned to respect time consciousness more, and I had to learn that it was sometimes convenient to be late. You soon discover that relationship is more important than being punctual."

This topic alone helped to move this couple away from "my way is the right way" to "I've learned one way; you have learned another. Let's glean from both and discover the best way for us."

An American woman married to a man from Scotland said, "The American way of life is a very independent one. In Scotland, the people in the community are much more aware of your presence, and they are more social. Family life is very different. It is a new way of thinking, and I had to discover the thought process of the new country I was now living in." Once she began to understand and appreciate the new way of thinking, she became very comfortable with this "foreign" country.

Caution Two: Be Accountable.

The second area of strong concern communicated by various couples interviewed was being certain that you are called together. "There is a tendency not to listen to people and the concerns they express about your possibility of marrying someone from a different culture," one spouse said. "It's easy to begin thinking, 'It's us against them,' and close yourselves to some very valuable input, confrontation, and honest hesitation provoked by these loved ones." In time, the goal can become a desire to beat the odds, prove the hesitant ones wrong, and press on ignorantly in order to make your point. Decide to be very accountable to your pastor, your parents, and to those whose relationship you value. Listen to them. Do not react by shutting them out. Weigh their concerns and think through their questions.

Caution Three: Know What Both Cultures Value.

In North American culture, there is a tendency to value things. In many other countries the tendency is to value extended family, the elderly, hospitality—a "what's mine is yours" type of mentality. People become the primary concern; consequently, what people think of you is important. One husband mentioned that his culture is more formal and conservative, especially in dress. "My wife," he explained, "is much more casual. In my country I wear long-sleeved dress shirts. They must be clean and pressed, or people will judge my spouse as a lazy wife."

One culture may value an education from the United States with such high regard that you would be expected to provide financially on a monthly basis for your extended family, as well as for others in need after completing your education. Other cultures value spontaneity. In the European world, more information and a lot of clarity is valued.

North Americans tend to discuss their feelings freely and may take the liberty to share their negative feelings with you. Central Americans may hide their feelings, especially those of anger or conflict. They desire everything to appear fine between you and them. The traditional values in East Africa would expect that cooking and caring for the children is totally the responsibility of the woman. Fathers may discipline the children, but not provide day-to-day care.

Caution Four: Identify Adaptation Versus Core Value Changes.

The final strong note of caution resulting from our survey concerned being aware of the difference between behavioral modification (or adaptation) and core value changes.

It is possible, for example, for a Middle Eastern man to adapt behaviorally to U.S. culture and look like he is indeed fitting into it. His core values may not have changed; he is simply conforming on the outside to the expectations of others. Because there is no inward change, this same man in his country of origin would sound like and think like a Middle Easterner. Why? In his thinking he has not lied or deceived—just adapted. He can now be who he really is and perform according to what he has been taught by his family and culture.

His unsuspecting wife finds herself living with a man whom she feels has made a radical about-face. She may feel trapped in a country and a culture with an unfamiliar person she once thought she knew.

Accept and Appreciate Differences

There will be times you may feel quite ready to argue that the way your culture does things is biblical. The point is that cultural differences exist, and you will be forced to face some of those mentioned and many that are not mentioned. If you choose to marry interculturally, you will need to learn to face cultural differences as a reality, not deny them.

Accepting and appreciating as many of the differences that you can will serve to enhance the marriage relationship. This experience is not to be viewed as all negative. The differences are something to embrace and value in one another. No two persons think alike or value the same things. You will need to give one another the freedom to be who you are and allow the Holy Spirit to mold your two cultures together. Rejoicing in the richness of your varied inheritances and learning from both can be a joyous experience.

Homesickness

Realistically, no matter where you live, one of you will miss home. Understand that one or both of you will have parents that feel separated from their son or daughter and, someday, grandchildren.

Visits to the home country of the spouse now living overseas can be very stressful. For example, there may be many relatives to visit within two short weeks! The foreign spouse may feel totally out of control in the situation. There is a larger than usual dependence on the spouse to drive the car, do business at the bank, and make decisions about other orders of business only known to the spouse in whose country of origin they are visiting. Allow time for acclimation to a new culture.

Also, one half of the extended family will only see the visiting spouse in a vacation setting and not in their normal lifestyle. This becomes an important area to communicate about for the couple and for their families of origin.

Keep in mind that there can be a time frame of several years between visits with family members. Saying good-bye after your visit home or after your family visits can be difficult. Some individuals found the time immediately following a family visit was when they battled homesickness, and even depression, the most.

Be Sure!

Miriam and Aaron, Moses' sister and brother, began to speak against Moses, "...because of his Cushite wife" (Num. 12:1). There may be those, even within your own family, who would speak against an intercultural marriage. You must prepare yourself for this added pressure and/or rejection. Do your best not to respond negatively to this criticism. Not everyone will understand or approve.

Ultimately it is God who calls two people together—not diversity of culture or a common missionary spirit. One couple stated it so well: "Be absolutely, positively sure it is God and not infatuation, rebellion, or some other emotion. Be in communication (with God and one another) at length, at all times, and at all costs!" In addition to what this couple emphasized, be in communication with and receive counsel from your pastor and/or spiritual authority.

The following exercises will help you to think through your own assumptions or prejudices. Realize that if you haven't discussed these areas with your premarital counselors, it is imperative to do so.

Intercultural Differences

Respond to each question or statement individually. Be sure to express yourself clearly and thoroughly.

1. Where will you live when you are married?
2. If you are from different countries of origin, have you experienced each other's country?
3. After marriage, how often do you plan to return to your country of origin for visits (or your spouse's country if you will be living in your country of origin)?
4. Have you established peace with your parents in this decision?
   Discuss your parents' reactions, hesitations, and encouragements.
5. Write about some cultural norms concerning male/female roles found within your country of origin.
6. What are some role differences that you notice now and know you will need to deal with in the future?
7. With two cultures merging into one, describe what steps you will take not to dictate your cultural norms to your spouse?
8. Describe how you hope your spouse will respond to you in terms of his/her cultural norms/expectations.
9. Have you discussed medical insurance and how it relates to the culture in which you plan to live? Have you shared your views on birth control with your future spouse?
   Do ideas about birth control present possible conflict?
   Yes _____ No _____
10. In some countries, children born to parents of different races are called "half-castes." How will you deal with prejudice toward your children?
11. Have you talked about where you want your children to be born?
    Yes _____ No _____
    If so, where and why?
    Have you discussed how many children you desire to have?
    Yes _____ No _____
12. Will your children be bilingual? Yes _____ No _____
13. If the country you will live in offers a lower educational standard, where will your children be educated?
14. During your engagement, how have you handled the challenges concerning intercultural marriage that you have received from others?
    Do you become defensive? Yes _____ No _____

Do you have a tendency to stick together and not deal with the challenge? Yes _____ No _____

15. How have you demonstrated realism in addressing the cultural differences that exist between you?

16. Can you describe for yourself and for your spouse what you feel will be some of the losses that will need to be faced (for example, living close to parents and family, conveniences, etc.)?
How do you tend to respond to the emotions created by these losses?

17. While living in a foreign country, with whom will you be in close relationship other than your spouse?

18. Do you have any friends or relatives in the country where you are presently living that can help hold you accountable through your engagement? Yes _____ No _____

19. Once you are married, are there any couples that you will be able to relate to and pray with concerning future needs and differences that may arise? Yes _____ No _____
If yes, who are they?

20. Take time to write about attitudes concerning work and attitudes concerning leisure from your culture. How do these attitudes differ from those of your future spouse?

21. Will you need to learn another language? Yes _____ No _____
Are you willing to study another language? Yes _____ No _____

22. Will you need visas? Yes _____ No _____
Where are you in the process of obtaining visas?
Will this process require a time of physical separation following marriage? Yes _____ No _____

23. Have you discussed medical needs?
What type of medical care is available in the country in which you will live? _____
What are the differences in medical care as compared to medical care offered in your country of origin?

24. Have you discussed your parents' roles after you are married?
Yes _____ No _____
Are there any differences of opinion concerning your or your future spouse's parental involvement in your marriage? Yes _____ No _____
Have you discussed extended family roles and involvement/responsibilities? Yes _____ No _____

25. Have you discovered any value differences concerning finances and budgeting? Yes _____ No _____
Discuss any differences discovered.

Have You Discussed...?

Complete the following exercise separately by placing a check under yes, no, or we need to discuss.

	Yes	No	We Need to Discuss
1. Food and meal preparation			
2. Home decorating			
3. Vacations as a couple and family			
4. The use of free time			
5. Celebration of important holidays			
6. Ways of educating children			
7. Dining out (how often/when)			
8. Spending money/allowance			
9. Spousal roles			
10. Ways of having fun			
11. Openness and the need for personal sharing			
12. Understanding of extended family			
13. Friendships within your fiancé/ée's culture			
14. Spiritual differences			
15. Missing home			
16. Separation from family and friends			
17. Standard of living			
18. Facing prejudice			
19. Roles and discipline of children			
20. New and different ways of doing things			
21. Facing suspicion			
22. History of each other's culture			
23. Differing musical tastes			
24. Perceptions of time			
25. Political views and participation			
26. Our tendencies to think my culture is "right"			
27. How we receive advice or counsel			

Scenario Communication

Please indicate how you will respond in the following situations.

1. You are not living in your country of origin. Your parents just left after a month-long visit. You feel like returning with them. How will you handle this emotional reaction?

2. You are pregnant with your first child and living away from your family of origin. You don't feel close to your in-laws who live in the same area as you. How will you adjust to these emotions?

3. You are living within your country of origin, which means your spouse is not. You begin to notice some depression in him/her and hear comments that would indicate homesickness. How will you adjust to these emotions?

4. Prior to marriage, your spouse agreed to live in your country of origin for a lifetime. You are now three years into the marriage, and he/she desires to move back to the country of origin. How will you handle this?

Intercultural Couple Dialogue

Locate a couple who are interculturally married and ask them if they would be willing to communicate with you and your future spouse about some of the differences they have discovered as an interculturally married couple. (Your pastor may be helpful in finding such a couple.) The following are suggested questions you can ask to generate dialogue between you as couples.

1. Could you share with us some of the positive experiences you have enjoyed as an intercultural marriage?

2. What are some of the negative experiences you've encountered?

3. Do you feel you've been able to uncover and deal with or replace the underlying assumption that my culture is "right"?

4. How does it feel for one of you to be living away from your family and country of origin?

5. How have you learned to appreciate the cultural differences?

6. What keeps your marriage strong in the midst of differences?

7. How do you prepare for and then handle visits to the home country of the spouse?

8. If one of you speaks a different language, how have you dealt with this?

9. What differences have you discovered concerning money and material things?

10. Can you share about your parents' involvement in your marriage?
11. What, if any, were areas of surprise to both of you?
12. If you met your spouse in your country of origin, can you discuss any differences that you discovered in your spouse when living in or visiting the country of origin?
13. If you could do some things over again, what changes would you make?
14. Would you advise a couple considering intercultural marriage to reside in a "neutral" country?

Personal Experience

As the two of you experience each other's country of origin and differences in culture before marriage, please discuss the positive and negative aspects of both.

1. When I experience my future spouse's culture, what I find to be positive is...
2. What could be considered negative for me is...
3. Something I have difficulty understanding is...
4. Some things that I saw as necessary for comfort in my country of origin that I will need to give up are...
5. Something I've enjoyed learning about my future spouse's culture is...
6. As I have experienced this "foreign" culture, some things that I have discovered about myself are...

Postmarital Checkup
for Interculturally Married Couples

1. What are some of the positive interculturally related experiences that you have had since marriage as a couple?
2. What are some of the exciting things that you have learned about an intercultural marriage?
3. Are there any negative experiences that you can share?
4. For the spouse who is living in a different country, what are some of the surprise experiences you were unprepared for?
5. How are your parents feeling about your marriage at this point in time? Are you pleased with their amount of involvement in your marriage?
6. How are you dealing with experiencing different cultural norms?

7. How are you helping one another to adapt to an intercultural marriage?

8. Do you have any close relationships with individuals or other couples presently? Is there another couple or pastoral person that you as a couple are accountable to?

9. Have your different backgrounds helped you develop friendships where you are living? Or, have these different backgrounds made it more challenging to develop friendships?

10. Are either of you having to learn another language? If so, share about your experience.

11. Have you discovered a work ethic that differs from your country of origin's work ethic?

12. Have you discussed your first visit to your partner's country of origin?

13. How can you be sensitive to your spouse when you are visiting your native country?

14. Are there any significant food and meal preparation differences between you as a couple?

15. What new or different ways of doing things have you discovered since marriage?

16. Has there been any role confusion (due to differing beliefs) since you married?

17. Have you discovered any cultural differences in the sexual realm of marriage?

18. Have you as an intercultural couple faced any prejudice where you are presently living?

19. In what ways are you having a tough time letting go of the idea that your way is right? How about your spouse? How do you think you can work further on this?

20. If you are not living in your country of origin, have you felt forced to adapt to an expectation of the culture that you are now residing in? Please explain.

21. Have you discovered any spiritual differences related to culture? ____

_____

22. Are there any other culturally related differences you have discovered? Please elaborate.

Interracial Marriages

Martin Luther King Jr. was once noted as saying that in America, Sunday morning has often been the most segregated hour of the week. Interestingly though, most Christians would voice that they do not believe it is right to be racist. Then why is it that many parents, siblings, relatives, and friends respond negatively to a person being interested in someone of another race? It seems that personal opinions can change when the subject gets close to home.

Take, for example, Jason and Traci. Traci shared with us, "We did have to deal with a family issue when we became engaged. My mom is concerned about our children. She is concerned that if we have kids, they could be black and darker than their father because Jason's dad is full African American. So my mom was worried that she could have black grandchildren and everyone would wonder how that happened and they might be treated differently. This was not a concern for Jason and me. Jason never felt any negative pressure growing up or had trouble fitting in due to the fact that his parents are from different races. But my mom grew up with a more conservative mindset, and for her this was a big deal. I also think the mindset was shared by my grandparents, although they were not as vocal with me. I ended up being a "shield" between Jason and my mom because I didn't want him knowing what she was upset about. But my knowing made me upset, and this added stress to our engagement."

What Does the Bible Say?

In the Old Testament, the Israelites were not to engage in mixed marriages (see Deut. 7:3-4). And then there is the story of the Tower of Babel (see Genesis 11:1-9) where many argue that God was actually separating the races. It is interesting, however, to discover that in Deuteronomy the reason Israelites were not to engage in interracial marriages was not because of racial differences, but simply that God did not want Israel to stray from Him into idol and pagan worship. When you look more carefully at the Tower of Babel you discover that the separation was about language and not race. God was never concerned about an "impure" race due to color, but His concern was a faith that was tainted with false beliefs.

Second Corinthians 6:14 warns us to not be yoked together with unbelievers. Why? Was it due to differing races? No. The Scripture clearly relates that to be married to an unbeliever would be like trying to mix light with darkness. The issue again is mixing the Christian faith with someone who would not value that faith and, in fact, would walk in sinfulness. The Bible does not say that interracial marriages are wrong. A theology based on racial separation causes skin color to become a priority that our heavenly Father never intended. It is our faith and belief in Christ as our Savior, and not our skin color, that is of greatest concern to God. That said, we must walk in wisdom, godly counsel, and prayer, rather than a spirit of "we will prove the naysayer wrong."

Some Statistical Data

According to a 1999 report in Cornerstone magazine, "Surveys conducted by the National Opinion Research Center of the University of Chicago have indicated that tolerance for interracial marriage relationships is increasing. In 1972, 39 percent of whites said that interracial marriages should be illegal; by 1991, the number had dropped to 17 percent. Acceptance of interracial marriage is higher among blacks, but by no means universal."[1] A 2007 Associated Press report indicated that since its legalization in America [*Loving* v. *Virginia*, 1967], there have been significant increases in interracial marriage—from 65,000 in 1970 to 422,000 in 2005. Stanford University sociologist Michael Rosenfield calculates that more than 7 percent of America's 59 million married couples in 2005 were interracial. Does this increasing tolerance mean that interracial marriages will soon suffer no negative consequences? "Not so," emphatically state the couples that we talked to. "Racial prejudice is alive and well today on the streets, in the neighborhood, in the mall, and in the church," said Jordon, a black man married to a white woman. "We experience prejudice a lot more than we would have ever imagined, and it seems no less painful with each occurrence."

Faith Binds Us Together

In the New Testament, Paul the apostle taught that Jesus had broken down any barrier between Jew and Gentile. It was Jesus who initiated conversation with the Samaritan woman (a culture "unclean" to the Jews) at the well. Christianity, more than any other faith, should bring the races together and not separate them. Moses was married to an "Ethiopian woman," and when Miriam, his sister, questioned Moses about this, the Bible tells us that she was struck with leprosy (see Num. 12). It would seem that God had a problem with Miriam's racism.

Interracial Cautions

Traci told us that when she experienced an interracial marriage, it opened new doors for her. She said, "You have the ability to adapt to new cultures more easily, and you tend to have friends of differing races which opens you up to many new relationships. You are not interacting with friends of one single race all the time. It truly is less boring." But the reality remains that interracial marriage also opens up doors of difficulties because of others who are not as accepting. Some will discriminate and ridicule. One person told us that this ridicule is the most difficult when it comes from your own family: "You know when someone is projecting shame."

Sometimes children of interracially married couples have different skin tones. Future grandparents need to be made aware of this.

Your interracial marriage may face difficulty in a neighborhood you choose to live in. One couple revealed to us that it took years of building relationships in their neighborhood until they felt any acceptance.

While it should not make a difference in the church you attend, you could experience negative feelings and unbiblical beliefs concerning interracial marriages.

These realities can put increased pressure on a young and vulnerable marriage relationship. The first year of marriage is challenging enough without facing interracial prejudice. Do not enter into this commitment without considering how you would deal with these possible challenges.

The Great News

The great news is that most likely you and your fiancé/ée have been grafted into the family of God by the cross of Christ. God's love knows no boundaries, and nothing can separate us from His love—not sin, not our race, not our skin color. Proceed in this process with wisdom and with prayer. Communicate thoroughly with one another and with your families. Do not separate yourselves from fellowship, but do choose to be part of a local church in which you are welcomed and supported as a couple. Your call together could be your opportunity to build some bridges throughout your lifetime of becoming one.

Interracial Questions to Consider

Please consider these questions separately.

1. Does your theology allow for an interracial marriage, and have you considered what God's Word has to say?
2. Discuss how you will deal with parents who do not approve of interracial marriage.
3. Can you be honest with your spouse about family feelings rather than hiding those reactions from him/her?
4. How have you had to face racial prejudice during your engagement, and can you give an example?
5. Have you thoroughly discussed bringing children into this marriage and what they may face? Please expound.

6. Do you believe that having an interracial marriage will make any difference in where you live, where you shop, where you fellowship, and perhaps where your children will attend school? Please write about your projections.

7. Do you relate to any other interracially married couples who you can ask questions of and receive input from? Give their names.

8. Do you know of any bridges that need to be built or rebuilt as an individual or as a couple? Please explain.

Additional Exercises

Persons experiencing interracial premarital counseling will also need to complete the following exercises from the "Intercultural Marriage" section of *Called Together*:

"Have You Discussed"

"Intercultural Couple Dialogue" (interchanging *interracial* for *intercultural*).

Endnote

1. *Cornerstone* 26, no. 111(1999).

Appendices

Are You on Schedule?

Check this wedding timetable.

- Discuss possible engagement with parents. Be sure of their approval.
- Discuss possible engagement with those in spiritual authority (pastor, associate pastor, premarital counselor, etc.).
- Seek counsel concerning an appropriate time frame for the wedding.

The Bride's Timetable
Six Months to One Year Before the Wedding

1. Discuss and set wedding budget with parents. Include groom and his parents in discussions if they are sharing costs.
2. Review, evaluate, and comparison shop for wedding sites. Select a wedding date, time, and place as soon as possible.
3. Start making guest list.
4. Plan color scheme for ceremony and reception.
5. Select and order wedding dress.
6. Choose attendants for wedding, and invite them to participate.
7. Reserve caterer, reception hall, photographer and/or video camera operator, and musicians.
8. Register at one or more stores for china, silverware, and other household items.
9. Purchase wedding ring for groom.
10. Choose wedding party attire for bridesmaids' dresses and mothers of bride and groom.

Three Months Before the Wedding

1. Complete guest lists and check for duplication.
2. Order invitations, enclosure cards, and personal stationery (for thank-you notes and future use).

3. Address invitations.
4. Groom and male attendants should select outfits.
5. Shop for trousseau.
6. Arrange for bridal portrait, if being taken ahead of time.
7. Arrange for tests for marriage license, if required.
8. Discuss ceremony and music with appropriate personnel.
9. Finalize reception plans.
10. Order wedding cake.
11. Order wedding flowers for bridal party, ceremony, and reception.
12. Mail invitations.

One Month Before the Wedding

1. Check guidelines for newspaper wedding announcements. Prepare the announcement, and send in when required.
2. Have final dress fitting.
3. Have wedding portrait taken.
4. Choose and order gifts for attendants.
5. Select gift for groom.
6. Arrange accommodations for out-of-town relatives and attendants.
7. Plan bridesmaids' party, if giving one.

Three Weeks Before the Wedding

1. Get marriage license with fiancé/ée.
2. Arrange transportation for bridal party to ceremony.
3. Discuss details of wedding and reception with photographer (or video camera operator).
4. Remind each member of the wedding party of the date, time, and place of rehearsal and wedding.

One Week Before the Wedding

1. Begin honeymoon packing.
2. Give or go to the bridesmaids' party; present gifts to attendants at bridesmaids' party or rehearsal dinner.
3. Provide final estimate of number of reception guests to caterer.
4. Check on final details with florist, photographer, and musicians.
5. Arrange to move wedding gifts and personal belongings to your new home.

The Groom's Timetable
Six months Before the Wedding

1. Order engagement and wedding rings for the bride.
2. Start guest list.
3. Select best man and other attendants (usually one usher for each 50 guests).
4. Discuss honeymoon plans with bride, and begin making arrangements.

Three Months Before the Wedding

1. Complete guest list; make sure addresses are correct.
2. Consult with bride about appropriate dress for you and male attendants.
3. Complete honeymoon plans and purchase tickets.
4. Consult with bride about flowers for bridal bouquet (usually paid for by groom).
5. Arrange accommodations for out-of-town relatives and ushers.

One Month Before the Wedding

1. Pick up wedding ring; check on engraving.
2. Help plan rehearsal dinner if your parents are hosting.
3. Select gift for bride.
4. Choose gifts for attendants. Make sure documents are in order (legal, medical, and religious).

Three Weeks Before the Wedding

1. Get marriage license.
2. Check on arrangements for bachelor dinner, if you are giving one.
3. Arrange for transportation to and from reception site.

One Week Before the Wedding

1. Remind best man and ushers of rehearsal time and place.
2. Present gifts to attendants.
3. Explain any special seating needs to head usher.
4. Get wedding clothes and going-away clothes ready.

Who Pays for What?

The following are general guidelines and not to be taken legalistically.

Bride

1. Wedding ring for the groom
2. Wedding gift for the groom
3. Gifts for the bridal attendants
4. Personal stationery
5. Medical examination and blood test, if required by law
6. Accommodations for out-of-town attendants

Groom

1. The bride's engagement and wedding rings
2. A wedding gift for the bride
3. Gifts for the best man and ushers
4. Groom's wedding attire
5. Bride's bouquet
6. Mothers' corsages
7. Boutonnieres for attendants and fathers
8. Medical examination and blood test, if required by law
9. Marriage license
10. Clergyman's fee
11. Honeymoon expenses
12. Bachelor dinner (if not given by the best man, optional)

Bride's Family

1. Engagement party (optional)
2. Ceremony cost: location, music, rentals and all related expenses
3. Entire cost of reception: food, beverages, entertainment, rental items, decorations, wedding cake
4. Bride's wedding attire and accessories

5. Wedding gift for the couple
6. Wedding invitations, announcements, and mailing costs
7. Bridesmaids' bouquets
8. Transportation for bridal party from bride's home to the site of ceremony
9. Bridesmaids' luncheon
10. Photography (groom's parents may pay for the pictures they would like)
11. Personal wedding attire
12. Floral decorations

Groom's Family

1. Rehearsal dinner party
2. Personal wedding attire
3. Travel and accommodations for groom's family
4. Wedding gift for the couple
5. Special items they may wish to purchase: toasting goblets, ring pillow, etc.
6. Any general expenses they may wish to contribute to

Birth Control

Children are a unique gift from God and provide a lifetime of blessing. The psalmist said, "Behold, children are a heritage from the Lord, the fruit of the womb is a reward....Happy is the man who has his quiver full of them..." (Ps. 127:3,5 NKJV). God has given us the ability to combine genes and see another human being with certain traits come forth. This "fruit" is the "heritage" that provides the "reward" of blessing to this new union.

God encouraged us in Genesis 1:28 to "be fruitful, and multiply; fill the earth" (NKJV). Therefore, marriage includes procreation. Some teach that a "quiver" contained five arrows. God leaves the decision concerning the number of children you give birth to up to you. Most Christians use some method of birth control, so we include a section on the subject. Each couple should pray and agree concerning the number of children they can train to serve God.

The following information was written by Scott Jackson, M.D. It is not all-inclusive but does provide a concise look at several methods of birth control. As a couple, pray, consult your physician, and educate yourselves. You may want to ask your doctor directly, "Is this method of birth control abortive?"

Many new types of birth control are now on the market. Most of these medications have a secondary action of changing the uterine lining so that it will not accept implantation by a fertilized ovum. This is abortive in nature. (Note—IUDs, intrauterine devices, are strictly abortive, in that, the primary action is to not allow any fertilized ovum to implant in the uterine wall.) There are certain types of oral contraceptives which would be considered abortive. We recommend that you discuss this important matter with your family physician or contact the National Right to Life with any questions. National Right to Life, Suite 402, 4197th Street NW, Washington, DC 20004; telephone 202-626-8800.

Options

Oral Contraceptives

Ovulation is directed by hormones, mainly estrogen and progesterone. Oral contraceptives consist of manmade versions of these hormones. They work to prevent the ovaries from producing eggs. Also, they help prevent sperm from reaching an egg. Several types of oral contraceptives exist with different levels of hormones. They also are available in 21-day or 28-day packs. Your doctor can determine which is right for you. Oral contraceptives are the most effective birth control method. Side effects are rare but can include headaches, weight gain, breast tenderness, and mid-cycle bleeding. There is a higher chance of blood clots or vascular disease, especially if one smokes while on the pill. The use of oral contraceptives must be monitored by a physician and must include yearly pap tests.

Diaphragm

The diaphragm is a soft rubber or latex cup that is inserted into the vagina to cover the cervix. It works as a barrier to sperm and is used with spermicidal jelly or cream, which kills sperm before they enter the uterus and fertilize the egg. The diaphragm will need to be fitted by your physician. He will instruct you on how to insert it and how to apply the spermicide. The diaphragm is highly effective if properly used. It must be inserted prior to intercourse each time. Afterward, it can be cleaned with soap and water. The diaphragm should be replaced every two years.

Spermicides

Spermicides kill sperm so that none can enter the uterus and fertilize an egg. They consist of jellies, cream, foam, or suppositories. When used with a diaphragm, they can be highly effective. Some use foam or suppositories without a diaphragm. They can be obtained without a prescription and are rather inexpensive. However, their effectiveness in birth control is not as high as the two previous methods mentioned.

Cervical Cap

The cervical cap is a smaller version of the diaphragm. It consists of a slightly thicker rubber and is filled with spermicidal jelly or cream. It should be fitted by your physician and must be rechecked yearly. The cervical cap is applied at the time of intercourse.

Condoms

The condom is a thin shield of latex that fits over the man's penis. It traps expelled semen during intercourse, preventing sperm from fertilizing an egg. The condom should be applied to the erect penis before intercourse. Afterward, he should withdraw immediately to prevent leakage. Condoms should be used in combination with spermicidal suppositories, jelly, cream, or foam as a backup form of birth control in case of leakage or breakage. Condoms, in general, are not as effective in birth control as the pill or diaphragm.

Contraceptive Sponges

The contraceptive sponge is a small, disposable, round, spermicide-containing sponge, which can be purchased over the counter. Use of the sponge can be fairly expensive because a new sponge must be used each time a couple has intercourse. Water is applied to the sponge, and it is inserted over the cervix. It does provide 24-hour protection and is about as effective as the diaphragm, except in women who have already had children.

Natural Family Planning

Natural family planning or "the rhythm method" utilizes the fact that fertilization is most likely to occur just before, during, or after ovulation. It is the least effective birth control method since even the most regular cycles can vary from month to month. The woman can monitor her ovulation schedule by checking her body temperature every morning and plotting it on a calendar for several months. She usually sees a slight rise in temperature during ovulation. Usually a pattern occurs, alerting the couple to avoid intercourse during the most fertile days. Most find that ovulation occurs 14 days before the start of the next menstrual period. Another way of determining ovulation is cervical mucus charting which involves observing a sample of mucus from the vagina daily. The mucus becomes clear, elastic, and slippery during ovulation.

Honeymoon Precautions

Sometimes new brides, especially those who are virgins, develop some painful, if not embarrassing, symptoms during or shortly after the honeymoon. We have included short descriptions of "honeymoon cystitis" and vaginitis as preventative information for the new bride and groom.

Cystitis

The urethra or tube draining urine from the bladder can be easily bruised, especially if not enough lubrication is provided for the penis to be inserted into the vagina. "Honeymoon cystitis" can result in bladder pain, bloody urine, or burning upon urination. Bruising of the urethra allows bacteria to grow in the urine stream causing an infection. This can easily be cured with antibiotic therapy and by drinking plenty of fluids. Repeated attacks can sometimes be prevented by urinating after each time of intercourse.

Vaginitis

Vaginitis, inflammation of the vagina, may have a host of causes. Usually, the woman will experience burning or unusual vaginal discharge. Sometimes painful intercourse results. She should seek medical attention in the event of any suspicion of vaginitis. There are over the counter preparations which promote effective cures; however, these should be used only under the recommendations of a physician. Some types of vaginitis can be passed from wife to husband and may require antibiotics for both partners.

Answers for Session Five:
Sexual Relations

Matching Questions

1.   T
2.   Z
3.   P
4.   J
5.   D
6.   C
7.   Y
8.   H
9.   N
10.   L
11.   B
12.   R
13.   F
14.   W
15.   A
16.   M
17.   I
18.   E
19.   Q
20.   K
21.   U
22.   S
23.   V
24.   X
25.   O
26.   G

Anatomy Questions
Male

8.	glans penis
3.	penis
4.	prostate gland
2.	scrotum
7.	seminal vesicles
1.	testicle
5.	urethra
6.	vas deferens

Female

1.	cervix
7.	clitoris
4.	Fallopian tube
6.	labia
3.	ovary
8.	urethra
5.	uterus or womb
2.	vagina

True or False Questions

1.	T
2.	T
3.	F
4.	T
5.	T
6.	F
7.	T
8.	T
9.	T
10.	F
11.	T
12.	T
13.	T
14.	T
15.	T
16.	F
17.	T
18.	F
19.	T
20.	F

Recommended Resource List

Additional books for instruction and reading pleasure:

Burkett, Larry. *Answers to Your Family's Financial Questions*. Pomona, CA: Focus on the Family, 1987.

Deal, Ron. *The Smart Stepfamily*. Grand Rapids, MI: Bethany House Publishers, 2002, 2006.

Dobson, Dr. James. *Love for a Lifetime*. Portland, OR: Multnomah Press, 1998.

Dobson, Dr. James and Shirley Dobson. *Night Light: A Devotional for Couples*. Sisters, OR: Multnomah Press, 2000.

Eggerichs, Emerson. *Love and Respect*. Nashville, TN: Thomas Nelson, 2004.

Feldhahn, Shaunti. *For Women Only*. Sisters, OR: Multnomah Publishers, Inc., 2004.

Feldhahn, Shaunti and Jeff Feldhahn. *For Men Only*. Sisters, OR: Multnomah Publishers, 2006.

Hart, Archibald. *The Sexual Man*. Dallas, TX: Word Pub., 1994.

Hart, Archibald, Catherine Weber, and Debra Taylor. *The Secrets of Eve*. Nashville, TN: Word Pub., 1998.

LaHaye, Tim and Beverly LaHaye. *The Act of Marriage*. Grand Rapids, MI: Zondervan, 1976.

Ludy, Eric and Leslie Ludy. *The First 90 Days of Marriage*. Nashville, TN: W Publishing Group, 2006.

McManus, Michael. *Marriage Savers: Helping Your Friends and Family Avoid Divorce*. Grand Rapids, MI: Zondervan, 1995.

Parrott, Les and Leslie. *Becoming Soul Mates*. Grand Rapids, MI: Zondervan, 1995.

Parrott, Les and Leslie. *Questions Couples Ask*. Grand Rapids, MI: Zondervan, 1996.

Penner, Clifford and Joyce Penner. *Getting Your Sex Life off to a Great Start*. Dallas, TX: Word Pub., 1994.

Prokopchak, Steve. *In Pursuit of Obedience.* Lititz, PA: House to House Publications, 2002.

Prokopchak, Steve. *Resolving Conflicts in Marriage.* Lititz, PA: House to House Publications, 2000.

Rainey, Dennis and Barbara Rainey. *Moments Together for Couples.* Ventura, CA: Regal Books, 1995.

Stoop, David and Jan Stoop. *When Couples Pray Together.* Ventura, CA: Regal Books, 2000.

Weber, Stu. *Tender Warrior.* Sisters, OR: Multnomah Publishers, 1999.

Wheat, Ed, MD. *Intended for Pleasure: Sexual Technique and Sexual Fulfillment in Marriage.* Old Tappan, NJ: Fleming H. Revell Co., 1977.

Wheat, Ed, MD, and Gloria Oaks Perkins. *Love Life for Every Married Couple.* Grand Rapids, MI: Zondervan, 1980.

Counselor's Guide Section

Counselor's Guide

Where can an engaged couple find clear, biblical premarital instruction? Did you and your spouse participate in any type of premarital counseling? We encourage you to take time to answer the following questions:

1. Did you and your spouse receive premarital counseling?
    Yes _____ No _____

2. Did your pastor require that you have premarital counseling?
    Yes _____ No _____

3. Who administered your premarital counseling?

4. How many sessions of counseling did you attend?

5. What were the topics discussed in each session?

6. Did you receive any homework assignments? Yes _____ No _____
    Did you complete the assignments? Yes _____ No _____

7. Were you assigned any books to read? Yes _____ No _____
    If yes, what were the book titles?

8. Did you complete any personality assessments or other tests?
    Yes _____ No _____

9. Were sexual relationships discussed to your satisfaction?
    Yes _____ No _____

10. Were finances discussed in detail? Yes _____ No _____

11. Rate your premarital counseling. (1 = inadequate, 10 = excellent)
    _____

12. How much effect did your premarital counseling have upon your marriage relationship? (1 = very little; 10 = very much) _____

While training local church couples to give premarital counseling, we asked some of these same questions. Many couples struggled to remember whether or not they had participated in premarital counseling. Some couples could not remember what content had been covered in their counseling.

One couple shared that they met with a psychologist for two premarital sessions. When asked why they attended only two sessions, they replied, "That's all we could afford." This is a sad testimony to the absence of the church in relation to training couples for marriage.

Where does a couple go for marriage training? The answer is obvious—to the church. Most couples desire to have a church wedding. However, many pastors have shied away from in-depth premarital counseling sessions for several reasons. One reason is the time commitment involved. Most pastors have tight schedules. Sadly, a second reason is the lack of comprehensive materials available to pastors.

Another question for pastors to consider is this: what is your philosophy concerning premarital education? Your philosophy will determine your premarital counseling process and the type of curriculum you use.

Called Together is unique in that it is administered couple-to-couple. We have successfully trained committed Christian couples rather than busy pastors to administer the pre- and postmarital instruction. They have committed themselves to work with a premarital couple for six or more sessions. This time frame allows for a quality relationship to develop, which continues through the postmarital sessions. Couples who desire to be married within our network of churches are required to participate in premarital counseling. Throughout the counseling process, they are challenged and encouraged. As the counselor couple studies the premarital material, they also become vulnerable and accountable to the couple they are counseling.

Let us share some reasons why we believe pre- and postmarital counseling is extremely important:

- Marriage was designed by God. We need to do our best to see each marriage built upon a proper foundation.
- Premarital counseling will expose potential problem areas. As these problem areas are exposed, they can be lovingly dealt with. This is preventative counseling at its best.
- Premarital counseling will build the faith of the couple, or it will reveal to the couple that they are, in fact, not called together. Note: We rarely refuse premarital counseling to anyone. However, we also make no promises to marry anyone. What we do, we must do in faith (see Rom. 14:23).
- Premarital counseling can be provocative and challenging.
- Premarital counseling helps the couple get their heads "out of the clouds," to face differences and reality.
- Postmarital counseling is a checkup and review, their first oil change, so to speak. Postmarital counseling within the first year of marriage provides opportunities for guidance, feedback, and prayer and nurtures a healthy environment in which to discuss troublesome areas of the marriage.
- Postmarital counseling reflects reality now that the couple has said, "I do." They now "know" one another. Faults and weaknesses have been exposed. The counseling couple can affirm strengths and encourage growth.

If we believe in strong, Christ-centered families, we must believe in and institute a thorough pre- and postmarital program.

This section of the book is a guide to the effective use of the *Called Together* pre- and postmarital program. *Called Together* is designed to provoke the couple to think and respond in writing. Each session will be approximately two hours long. Confidentiality on the part of both couples is essential. Disclosure is vital, and details should not be discussed outside of the counseling sessions without permission.

Counselor couples must be willing to share about their marriage and provide a godly role model. They must also be willing to talk about difficult areas within the marriage relationship. They cannot be embarrassed to discuss such topics as childhood, family of origin issues, sexual foreplay, salvation, and so forth. Counselor couples need to be able to ask pertinent questions. Dependence upon the Spirit of God is essential. The Holy Spirit can reveal hidden areas such as family curses, previous sexual involvement, past physical, emotional, or sexual abuse, or unhealthy relationships from the counselee's past. Counselor couples must not be afraid to confront sin in a loving manner.

The remainder of this section provides specific directions for each counseling session. Personalize each session according to the particular couple's needs. Pray with the couple frequently. Be sure to maintain accountability in all areas, with special focus on the couple's physical relationship while they are engaged. God bless you as you provide thorough pre- and postmarital counseling to better equip couples for a lifelong commitment to marriage.

Premarital Sessions

The following instructions will help you initiate the premarital training efficiently and with confidence. *Called Together* is best administered couple-to-couple. Consequently, a relationship will develop that could carry on throughout the new marriage. Before your first counseling session, the engaged couple should receive the *Called Together* books and complete the "Premarital Counseling Identification Data" as well as "Session One: About Me" homework exercises.

Important: All assignments are to be completed and turned in to you, the counselor, before your first meeting with the couple. This will facilitate review of their recorded answers and help prepare you to personalize the sessions according to their needs as a couple. Assignments for the remaining sessions should also be completed and in your possession *before* the corresponding counseling session. While conducting premarital counseling, we have collected the counselee's books Sunday morning for a Monday night session, and we have found books hanging on our front door knob, on porch furniture, or coming to us via overnight mail.

It may be advisable to meet with the couple before initiating any premarital sessions. During this time you should assess their relationship with God and whether or not God is calling you to be involved in their premarital training. For those who are equipped not only to give premarital training, but also to perform the actual marriage ceremony, it would be advisable to tell the couple that being involved in premarital counseling is no guarantee that you will perform the wedding ceremony. Performing the actual ceremony is something that God must give you faith for only after He has confirmed the couple and their call together.

We recommend giving a copy of the book *Love Life for Every Married Couple* by Ed Wheat to the couple at the beginning of the premarital counseling. A copy of the book *Getting Your Sex Life Off to a Great Start* by Dr. Clifford and Joyce Penner can be given when you sense that it is appropriate for the couple to begin reading about sexual relations. The books should be read by the counselees before the last session of counseling. (An exception may be *Getting Your Sex Life Off to a Great*

Start. Some couples have expressed difficulty with their physical relationship due to the explicit nature of the material covered in this book.)

In *Called Together,* appendix A and appendix B, you will find helpful resources for the couple to use in the planning stage of the wedding. Birth control information is available in appendix C, and appendix D offers honeymoon precautions.

Premarital Course Overview

A. **Goals of Premarital Training**
    1.   To introduce the couple to God's institution of marriage
    2.   To thoroughly prepare a couple for marriage

B. **Sub-goals of Premarital Training**
    1.   To assist the couple in taking an honest look at themselves
    2.   To help the couple evaluate their present relationship
    3.   To improve communication skills
    4.   To aid in the development of financial skills and financial accountability
    5.   To provide accurate and appropriate information in the area of sexual relations
    6.   To aid the couple in ceremony planning

C. **Objectives of Premarital Training Will Be Met By:**
    1.   Attending at least five premarital sessions and one marriage ceremony planning session.
    2.   Studying scriptural marriage concepts.
    3.   Observing aspects of marriage exemplified by couple counselors.
    4.   Completing reading and writing assignments.
    5.   Completing a personality profile.
    6.   Participating in open discussion, Bible study, and prayer.

About Me
Premarital Session One

To prepare couples for a God-honoring and personally satisfying relationship in marriage, an initial marital readiness assessment should be conducted. To assist the counselors, spiritual overviews of both individuals and "About Me" worksheets are included in the assignments for Session One. Discuss the intent of these worksheets in Session One to help determine potential spiritual conflict or compatibility. Responses to the "About Me" questions will reveal a wealth of individual reactions to anger, fear, guilt, and so forth. Realistically speaking, many couples never see beyond the "nice" side of their future spouse. To be prepared to face difficulties or conflicts in marriage, couples should be better informed about the "other" side of their future spouse.

Session One is the time to administer a personality tool which you have been trained to use. There are a number of excellent tools: the Taylor Johnson test, the Myers-Briggs, the DISC. Make use of a tool that you and your pastoral leader are most familiar with. You may give the results to the couple in Session Two or throughout the premarital sessions. However you choose to use this tool, be considerate and wise when revealing the information to the couple.

A scriptural review of love should be included in Session One. The exercise "A Biblical Concept of Love" offers a basis for this discussion. Wedding timetables found in appendix A are included to assist the couple in making plans for their wedding, and a handout entitled "Who Pays for What?" (appendix B) will help clarify financial obligations.

It will be important as counselors to address the individual responses to the exercise "Individual Mission." Frequently, singles make marriage their goal. Marriage is not the goal, but rather, seeing the individual calls of God in their lives joined to become a cooperative mission. Are their individual missions compatible, or are they too diverse to be united? An example of diverse missions could be the following: Don senses a strong call of God to minister to inner city youth while Beth, having participated in several short-term mission trips, feels a strong leading toward foreign missions. Are these missions compatible? Can they become compatible?

The mission exercises in Sessions One and Two will help you as counselors and the engaged couple to assess the plausibility of the prospective marriage mission. Remember, do not make any assumptions concerning this couple. Treat them as if they know nothing about marriage preparation even if one or both have been previously married.

For a spiritual overview, you will want to discuss the following topics and Scriptures:

Salvation	John 3:3; Romans 10:9
Sin	Romans 3:10,23
Lordship	Luke 14:33
Water Baptism	Matthew 28:19; Acts 16:33
The Holy Spirit	Matthew 3:11; Acts 1:8
Prayer	Luke 18:1; 1 Thessalonians 5:17
The Word	Psalm 119:11,105; Ephesians 6:17; Hebrews 4:12
Church Attendance	Hebrews 10:25

Finally, and of extreme importance, discuss purity with the couple. Consider these areas:

1. Seek God first (see Matt. 6:33).
2. Commit yourselves to purity (see 1 Tim. 5:1-2).
3. Be committed to communication so as to not defraud one another (see Eph. 4:15).
4. Be committed to accountability with parents, pastor, and counselors (see James 5:16).
5. Be sure to address the sexual boundaries assignment and follow through with personal accountability for this couple in this most vulnerable area. They will need you to ask them the difficult questions of boundary keeping. Pursue this topic prayerfully throughout your time of premarital counseling.

About Us
Premarital Session Two

Many couples enter marriage unrealistically. God wants us to be full of faith but "wise as serpents." With the great wealth of literature, videos, and audio tapes available on the subjects of marriage, sex, finances, communication, and so forth, no couple should enter marriage unaware of satan's devices to undermine and destroy relationships.

Reasons for marriage can vary widely. The exercises "Reasons for Marriage" and "Expectations and Perceptions of Marriage" help the counselors and the couple sift through the emotional and romantic issues to determine the valid call of God to marriage. Is this couple compatible in the expectations and perceptions of marriage? Potential areas of conflict could be identified as you review both sets of expectations in your counseling session. Be careful not only to point out potential problem areas, but also the positives from areas of agreement. Point the couple to Scripture passages that provide answers for possible conflicts.

Normally, engaged couples will have the following three expectations:
1. They expect that this marriage will never end in divorce.
2. They expect faithfulness and commitment from each other.
3. They expect minimal adjustments and few, if any, problems.

Be aware that when expectations are not met they can become demands. Please share some of your premarital and postmarital expectations that were not met by your partner and how you dealt with these unmet expectations.

The exercise on reactions deals with "what if" situations. Hopefully the couple will not have to face any of these situations. But what if...? Use God's Word to address these situations, offering God's hope for any problem that could arise.

The next exercise in Session Two provokes discussion about parents. Family of origin issues are an essential topic for premarital counseling. Does the couple have their parents' blessing? Take the time to discuss this exercise. Be aware that these questions cannot possibly cover every issue that pertains to the family of origin. Cover the exercise "Are You Ready to Leave and Cleave?" thoroughly with the engaged couple.

Let's Talk
Premarital Session Three

Effective communication is vital to a stable, intimate, and satisfying marriage relationship. A breakdown of communication is almost always a primary cause of marital dysfunction. Ed Cole states that when communication stops, abnormality sets in, and the ultimate end of abnormality is death of the relationship. Just as faith dies when we refuse to communicate with our heavenly Father, so will a marriage die when a couple refuses to communicate. Ephesians 4:29-30 reveals that the purpose of communication is to edify, not corrupt. The Holy Spirit is grieved when we are not ministers of grace as we communicate with one another.

The varied assignments for this session cover communication extensively—nonverbal communication, communication guidelines, effective communication, scenario communication.

Our communication goals include the following: to share with one another freely, to be lovingly honest about what we think and feel, to understand each other, to listen respectfully and respond appropriately, to be able to disagree and discuss our disagreements without becoming hurt or attacking one another, to have conversation that is beneficial and uplifting.

Norm Wright, in his book *Training Christians to Counsel*, states that communication is made up of the following components:

7 percent words (content)

38 percent attitude (tone of voice)

55 percent body language

It will be vital for you to emphasize the importance of healthy communication. As you and the couple work together, you will have the opportunity to refer to unhealthy methods of communication, as well as the tone of voice and body language employed by the counselees.

James 4:1-2 informs us that conflicts come from wanting something but not getting it. In order to help the couple work through possible communication difficulties, the following synopsis for conflict resolution should be helpful.

A. **Decision-making is a large part of the conflict resolution process.**
    Ask: Who made the decisions in their families of origin?
    Who will exert more influence in decision-making in this new family?
    Who will ultimately be responsible for decisions made?
    How has the couple been making decisions independently?
    How have they been making decisions during their engagement period?
    How have they escaped decision-making in the past?

B. **Take practical steps to resolve conflict. (Remember, when conflict comes, you tend to focus on yourself.)**
1.   Don't demand; listen (see Prov. 18:13).
2.   Select the right time and place (see Prov. 15:23).
3.   Define the problem area.
4.   Define the areas of agreement and disagreement.
5.   Identify your contribution to the problem—accept some responsibility.
6.   Identify the behaviors you need to change.
7.   Listen to the feelings of the other person. (Feelings do not need to be factual; however, you can agree that your spouse is "feeling" this way.)
8.   Find out what the Word of God says about the problem area.
9.   Pray together and agree on necessary changes.

Covering the following verses will be helpful: Proverbs 13:18; 23:12; 25:12; 28:13; Philippians 3:13.

Finances
Premarital Session Four

Conflicting ideas about finances often cause marital dysfunction. In many of the divorces filed each year in our country, complaints often involve finances. God gives clear guidelines and principles for handling finances in His Word. Truth about finances can be found in Scripture.

Also included in this session are assignments which will clarify personal views about finances and a budget profile. Take time to cover the budget profile with the couple. Be sensitive to any potential problems in the financial area. (It is recommended that you as counselors familiarize yourself with this budget profile by inserting your personal financial figures and personally working through the process.)

In Session Four, you will want to discuss financial expectations. For example, a couple may expect to purchase a new home within the first year of marriage; they may need to buy a second car or decide to replace one of their present vehicles with a newer one; they may unconsciously expect to be at the financial level of their parents or another couple whom they admire before that can be a reality. It will be important for you as counselors to confront these financial issues candidly.

As mentors, you have the opportunity to guide this couple toward trusting God for their finances rather than trusting credit cards, loans, or family members. Prayerfully consider sharing Luke 12:22-31 with the couple. God is their source.

Sexual Relations
Premarital Session Five

God is the creator of sex. He originated lovemaking between married partners. Sex is a beautiful and intimate relationship shared uniquely by a husband and wife.

In His Word, God has given information and directions concerning sexual relations. He doesn't consider sex an embarrassing topic. He addresses marriage in a discreet and wholesome way. As counselors, we need to follow God's lead. We need to be sources of helpful and practical information. Many couples go into marriage unprepared, naïve, and sadly misinformed about sexuality and sexual relations. Many Christian marriages are lacking vitality and are less than God's best, leaving unfulfilled partners to continue without hope of change.

Homework exercises found in this session will open up discussion on attitudes and beliefs about sex, provide scriptural references to sex in marriage, and include matching definitions of sexual terms, identification of male and female anatomy, and true/false statements regarding areas of sexuality. (Answers to these final three exercises are found in appendix E.) Assess the couple's abilities to express themselves about sex; are they embarrassed, fearful, disgusted, naïve, or do they use inappropriate terminology? Use Scripture to address any misguided attitudes. Offer practical advice for the honeymoon (see appendix D). Reassure the couple that you will be available for counsel in the postmarital relationship.

Marriage Ceremony Planning
Premarital Session Six

The exercises in this section are extremely important for the premarital counselors, as well as the minister who will perform the ceremony. If you have served a couple through premarital counseling, but you are not going to perform the marriage ceremony, you will need to give your input and assessment to the minister. If your assessment of this couple is that they are not prepared for marriage, or if you believe that they are premature in their call together, then they must be lovingly advised.

Take special note of the exercise "Saying I Do" in Session Six in the Premarital Section. Your emphasis should be on the spiritual union that occurs during a marriage ceremony. Please familiarize yourself with these areas. You may encourage the couple to discuss some of the points with their parents. After the sample ceremony, take a realistic look at the honeymoon, and ask the couple some candid questions. The honeymoon is an important part of the wedding planning. Take time to walk the couple through their expectations of this event.

The final exercise in this chapter is a study on "submission," a very misunderstood topic in the Church today. It is our belief that this study is simple, clear, theologically sound, and very helpful in comprehending the topic. As counselors, be clear on the biblical definition and scriptural references to submission. Be prepared to give examples of submission from your mission together as premarital counselors and share how submission has developed in your relationship. (Suggestion: Share with the couple how giving pre- and postmarital training is a cooperative mission, one which gives you the opportunity to submit to one another.)

It is very important that the couple enjoys each aspect of the planning—from choosing invitations, gowns, and flowers to writing their vows and making arrangements for the honeymoon. Caution the couple not to allow themselves to become anxious or frustrated with details. This is a one-time experience, and they will be grateful for happy memories.

Postmarital Session

Postmarital Course Overview

A. Goals of Postmarital Training

1. To reinforce premarital instruction and implementation of that information
2. To provide an assessment of the positive growth within this new marriage
3. To focus on specific or potential problem areas within this marriage

B. Sub-goals of Postmarital Training

1. To aid the couple in evaluating their present relationship
2. To provide helpful dialogue between the newly married couple and the postmarital counselors
3. To aid the couple in the further development of spiritual skills, communication skills, financial skills, and sexual skills

C. Objectives of Postmarital Training Will Be Met By:

1. Attending at least two postmarital sessions.
2. Re-administering the personality profile.
3. Reviewing appropriate premarital information.
4. Modeling/dialoguing aspects of the marriage relationship with the couple and counselors.
5. Completing reading and writing assignments.
6. Participating in prayer and Bible study.

Counselor's Guide
Before Postmarital Sessions

A general guideline for postmarital counseling would be to meet with the couple at three months and nine months after the wedding. The postmarital course is designed with a minimum of two sessions in mind. You may meet with this couple as often as necessary. Note that the areas of review in this guide are divided into two sessions. Discuss "Spiritual Overview" and "Communication Overview" at the three-month session. "Financial Overview" and "Sexual Overview" can be reviewed at the nine-month session.

It is assumed that you were the couple's premarital counselors. If you did not perform the premarital counseling, then have a get-acquainted session. In this meeting you will need to gather as much background information as possible. You could use your *Called Together* book as an outline for questioning.

Require the couple to turn in their *Called Together* three-month postmarital assignments before the scheduled session. You will also want them to bring their relational profiles. If you are certified to administer a profile, you will want to re-administer it to the couple and note any personality/behavior differences in their graphs. It is extremely profitable to profile the couple during the postmarital training.

We recommend that the book *The First 90 Days*, by Eric and Leslie Ludy, be given to the newlyweds at the first postmarital session and completed by the last session.

The second set of exercises are to be completed and turned in to you before the nine-month session. This will give you time to review the couple's responses and make note of specific areas for discussion.

Build upon the relationship that you established during the premarital course now in the more realistic postmarital counseling sessions. Always keep in mind that counseling couples toward a Christ-centered marriage will influence their children and generations to come. Your example, warmth, love, confrontation, empathy, and understanding translate into the act of "equipping the saints for the work of ministry" (Eph. 4:12). There is no greater ministry than serving and building the Christian family!

Three Months
Postmarital Session One

A. **Spiritual Overview**
1. Where is the couple in their relationship with Jesus Christ? Is this couple: attending church as a couple, involved in daily couple devotions, involved in daily individual devotions, praying with one another, tithing and giving to others?
2. What are their spiritual goals (for example, being involved in short-term missions or long-term missions, leading a home fellowship group, ministering to others)?
3. What will help to make this couple spiritually successful? Please cover the following verses with the couple.
    a. **Our sufficiency is in Christ.** "Not that we are sufficient of ourselves to think of anything as being from ourselves, but our sufficiency is from God who also made us sufficient as ministers of the new covenant, not of the letter but of the Spirit; for the letter kills, but the Spirit gives life" (2 Cor. 3:5-6 NKJV).
    b. **Be effective and productive Christians.** "But also for this very reason, giving all diligence, add to your faith virtue, to virtue knowledge, to knowledge self-control, to self-control perseverance, to perseverance godliness, to godliness brotherly kindness, and to brotherly kindness love. For if these things are yours and abound, you will be neither barren nor unfruitful in the knowledge of our Lord Jesus Christ. For he who lacks these things is shortsighted, even to blindness, and has forgotten that he was cleansed from his old sins" (2 Peter 1:5-9 NKJV).
        "For where your treasure is, there your heart will be also" (Matt. 6:21).
    c. **We need not fear; He holds the future.** "There is no fear in love; but perfect love casts out fear, because fear involves torment. But he who fears has not been made perfect in love" (1 John 4:18 NKJV).
        "Brethren, I do not count myself to have apprehended; but one thing I do, forgetting those things which are behind and reaching forward to those things which are ahead....Be anxious for nothing, but in everything by prayer and supplication, with thanksgiving, let your requests be made known to God" (Phil. 3:13; 4:6 NKJV).

    d.   **Trust and know God.** "Trust in the Lord with all your heart, and lean not on your own understanding; in all your ways acknowledge Him, and He shall direct your paths" (Prov. 3:5-6 NKJV). "All things are possible to him who believes" (Mark 9:23 NKJV). "Behold, I am the Lord, the God of all flesh. Is there anything too hard for me?" (Jer. 32:27 NKJV). "Thus says the Lord: 'Let not the wise man glory in his wisdom, let not the mighty man glory in his might, nor let the rich man glory in his riches; but let him who glories glory in this, that he understands and knows Me, that I am the Lord, exercising loving kindness, judgment, and righteousness in the earth. For in these I delight,' says the Lord" (Jer. 9:23-24 NKJV).

    e.   **Be a doer.** "But be doers of the word, and not hearers only, deceiving yourselves. For if anyone is a hearer of the word and not a doer, he is like a man observing his natural face in a mirror..." (James 1:22-23 NKJV).

B.   **Communication Overview**

    1.   Have the couple turn to the "Perceptions of My Spouse" in the Postmarital Section, Session One: Three Months. How has the couple dealt with the expectations about which they previously wrote? Are there new areas of expectation?

    2.   Review the practical steps to resolve conflict found at the end of the "Communication" section of the Counselor's Guide along with James 4:1-2. Review Norm Wright's analysis of communication. Ask the couple to share how they have been resolving conflicts.

    3.   What has the couple discovered about nonverbal communication? Are there any ways in which a spouse has experienced negative nonverbal communication? Discuss this.

    4.   Review "Communication Guidelines."

    5.   Review appropriate "Have You Discussed...?" questions. (For example, is the couple showing their feelings and attitudes, differences, and hurts without anger and criticism?)

    6.   Assignment: Reread Chapter 11, "The Secret of Staying in Love" (especially for newlyweds), in the book *Love Life for Every Married Couple* by Dr. Ed Wheat.

Note: Are you accountable in these areas? Be certain that your marriage is a Christ-centered, positive example to the couple you are counseling.

Nine Months
Postmarital Session Two

A. Financial Overview

1. Review "Personal Financial Views" in Session Four of the Premarital Section. How have the couple's premarital views changed? Cover again all 19 questions.

2. Take the couple through a review of the "Scriptural Truths About Finances." Are they walking in accordance with God's Word in the financial realm?

3. Is the couple using the "Personal Finances Budget Sheet" or are they keeping records with a different tool? Ask the couple to complete a new budget sheet. They can use the line item instructions found in the postmarital material.

4. Thoroughly review their financial status. Are they tithing? Do they have concrete places in which to invest for their future (IRA, retirement, real estate)? Do they live in a high rent area? Is their rent within their budget? Carefully look over the utilities. How much is their monthly telephone bill? Are long distance calls within reason? Has the couple incurred new debt? Is a vehicle payment restricting them financially? Are they spending money for date nights? Is the couple overinsured/underinsured? Is the couple saving for annual or semi-annual bills? Are their present bills current?

5. Question whether or not this couple is walking in financial agreement. Are they accountable to one another in their spending? Do they give one another an allowance? If there is a financial need, are they willing to trust God to meet that need?

6. Can this couple live on the husband's salary or are they depending upon the wife's income as well? Discuss this thoroughly along with their financial goals. Ask the couple how their goals may change when children arrive.

7. Pray for God's blessing on their finances. Share with them that God is their Provider. The ultimate Source is not their jobs, the bank, the church, or their parents.

Note: Keep in mind that as a more experienced couple you can help hold this couple accountable with their finances, if they wish. A review of their financial status and financial goals will indicate how realistic this couple is in relation to their income and expenditures.

B. **Sexual Overview**

1. Go over appropriate "Questions for Discussion" (questions 2, 4, 5, 6, and 11) in Session Five in the Premarital Section.

2. What attitudes or beliefs about sex have surfaced since the wedding night?

3. What sexual complications has the couple encountered? Are they both experiencing orgasm? Are they free to communicate their sexual needs with one another?

4. Thoroughly review "A Creative Plan" in Session Five: Premarital Section. Does this couple have any questions about lovemaking? Remind them that this is an area they will grow in and that sex is about giving, not taking.

5. Does the couple have any questions concerning birth control? See appendix C. Have their plans for having children changed now that they are married?

Assignment: Reread chapters 6, 11, 13, in Dr. Ed Wheat's book *Love Life for Every Married Couple.*

Note: Be sure to remind the couple to read the book *Getting Your Sex Life Off to a Great Start* by Dr. Clifford Penner as a helpful reference.

Additional Wisdom

Five additional sections are provided in *Called Together* that help you to customize and serve the many different marriage scenarios you may face as counselors. These sections must be completed concurrently with the other pre- and postmarital material found within this book.

It is important to point out that your theology plays a key part in couples remarrying. Today biblical guidelines can often take a back seat to personal desires. As Christian counselors we need to keep God's truth in the forefront even though it may go against what a couple wants or thinks they need. The truth of God's Word must supersede personal desire.

Please keep in mind that different cultures can reflect very different ideas. We must recognize that different is not necessarily wrong. While Jesus transcends culture, culture does not change God's Word.

We have attempted throughout these sections to give to you a biblical understanding of remarriage versus personal beliefs and doctrines. Naturally, we tend to think that our beliefs and our culture along with our denomination's theology is the most correct. You, as counselors, must be willing to listen objectively without passing judgment, refrain from projecting personal beliefs, and keep an open mind to differing perspectives. We will never be able to help these couples through their challenges if we cannot embrace such a mindset.

Counseling Schedule

Use this schedule to plan and keep track of your counseling appointments.

Premarital Session	Date	Time	Place
1			
2			
3			
4			
5			
6			
Postmarital Session			
1			
2			

Seminar, Retreat, or Workshop Presentations

Steve and Mary Prokopchak
11 Toll Gate Road, Lititz PA 17543
Telephone: 717-627-1996
E-mail: info@dcfi.org

About the Authors

God called Steve and Mary together in marriage over 33 years ago. It has always been their heart to have a marriage built on Christ and to help others to do the same. From raising a family of three children, to counseling, writing, and speaking, they have endeavored to help marriages thrive in a way that honors the Creator of marriage.

Mary is a registered nurse and still works part time in her field. Steve, as a member of the Apostolic Council of DOVE Christian Fellowship International (DCFI), helps provide oversight and direction for DCFI churches in the United States, Caribbean, and New Zealand. He also serves on the USA Team of DCFI and the International Advisory Apostolic Group. A Christian family and marriage counselor for many years, Steve earned his Master's of Human Services degree from Lincoln University.

It is Steve and Mary's personal vision and hearts' cry to see people made whole in their personal lives, marriages, and families. Countless individuals have been affected through Steve and Mary's training, whether one-on-one or during seminars, conferences, marriage retreats, and written materials. They travel regularly, ministering in churches across the nation and internationally equipping people with various leadership and counseling tools.

Steve and Mary wrote *Called Together,* a unique book specifically designed for couple-to-couple mentoring. Steve also authored a series of booklets called *People Helping People* on counseling topics suitable for small groups. He coauthored *The Biblical Role of Elders for Today's Church* and is the author of *In Pursuit of Obedience.* Steve has had articles published in *Charisma* magazine, *Ministries Today,* and *Cell Group Journal.*

OTHER RESOURCES BY STEVE PROKOPCHAK

Called Together **Counselor's Training Audio**
Marriage, It's God's Plan

This CD set is based on the material in Called Together, a unique book designed for couple-to-couple mentoring use, preparing couples for a successful marriage. The informative sessions train church leaders and lay couples for pre- and postmarital counseling. Valuable insights are provided to draw a couple out so they can take a thorough look at themselves, their backgrounds, and their future. CD Set with Steve & Mary Prokopchak.

Helpful tracts
"Who I Am in Christ"
"Praying for My Spouse"
"Praying for My Children"
Provoke biblical change through prayer. Dozens of
Scriptures provide prayer points to motivate change from the inside out.
Available in 10, 50, and 100-packs.

Counseling Basics
This material is specifically geared to train small group
leaders, assistant leaders, and youth leaders to counsel others.
Packed with helpful scriptural references. Covers 18 essential areas.
Workbook, *112 pages*
Audio set of six tapes or CDs

In Pursuit of Obedience
God's love must be the foundation for building emotional,
physical, and spiritual health. Yet how do we obey God when it is
uncomfortable? Ideal for small group study with discussion and activities.
80 pages

People Helping People Series
With examples and illustrations, discussion questions
and outlines, this series is helpful for small group
study, one-on-one mentoring, or as a teaching resource.

Emotional Dependency

Identifies and deals with emotionally dependent relationships.
Solutions and assignments help to further reveal how a
person can be free of dependent relationships. *32 pages*

Thinking Right

If you want to cling to your past, this information is not for you.
If you want to move on in your Christian walk, this booklet helps you
analyze and gives scriptural support about the process of change. *36 pages*

Be Angry and Sin Not

Do you make excuses for your anger or for the anger of another?
Have you been affected by an angry person? Includes biblical
insights into how to make changes or help someone else. *36 pages*

Resolving Conflicts in Marriage

Do your expectations in marriage turn into demands? Have you taken
a passive role, resulting in a drifting apart of the relationship? Learn how
to reverse this trend and build the life of Christ in your spouse. *48 pages*

For more about these resources, visit www.h2hp.com.

Additional copies of this book and other
book titles from DESTINY IMAGE are
available at your local bookstore.

Call toll-free: 1-800-722-6774.

Send a request for a catalog to:

Destiny Image® Publishers, Inc.
P.O. Box 310
Shippensburg, PA 17257-0310

*"Speaking to the Purposes of God for This
Generation and for the Generations to Come."*

**For a complete list of our titles,
visit us at www.destinyimage.com.**